# Money, Prices, and Civilization in the Mediterranean World

*FIFTH TO SEVENTEENTH CENTURY*

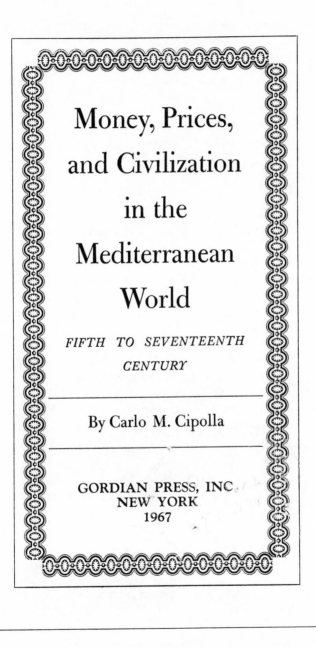

# Money, Prices, and Civilization in the Mediterranean World

*FIFTH TO SEVENTEENTH CENTURY*

By Carlo M. Cipolla

GORDIAN PRESS, INC.
NEW YORK
1967

Carlo M. Cipolla is professor of economic history at
the Istituto Universitario di Economia e Commercio
in Venice. He has studied not only in his native Italy
but in France and Britain, with scholarships from
the governments of those two countries, and he has
taught at the Universities of Pavia, Catania, and
Genoa. In the United States he has lectured at the
Universities of Cincinnati and Wisconsin and at Yale
and the Johns Hopkins Universities; in Europe at
Cambridge, Oxford, and North Staffordshire Universities, and at the Universities of Ghent and Lille. His
published works include books in Italian and French,
and numerous articles in those languages and English.

Published by GORDIAN PRESS, INC., with the permission
of Princeton University Press. 1967

Library of Congress Catalog Card Number 67-18440

Printed in U.S.A. by
EDWARDS BROTHERS, INC.
Ann Arbor, Michigan

TO MY FRIENDS AND COLLEAGUES IN
THE UNIVERSITY OF CINCINNATI
THE UNIVERSITY OF WISCONSIN
THE JOHNS HOPKINS UNIVERSITY
YALE UNIVERSITY
IN GRATITUDE FOR THEIR GENEROUS
HOSPITALITY

*En monnoies est li cose*
*moult obscure*
*Elles vont haut et bas*
*se ne set-on que faire*
*Quand on guide wagnier*
*on troeve le contraire*
*(Gilles Li Muisis, abbot of*
*St. Martin's in Tournai,*
*fourteenth century)*

## PREFACE

The five chapters of this volume represent five lectures given at the University of Cincinnati under the auspices of the Charles Phelps Taft Memorial Fund.

It was not intended in the lectures to give a complete and systematic survey of the history of money and prices in the Mediterranean world from the fifth to the seventeenth century. Within the limits allowed, such a presentation would have been decidedly superficial and unsatisfactory. Instead it seemed preferable to select and discuss single topics which in the opinion of the author are especially significant for the whole subject.

Among those to whom the author is indebted are first of all the members of the Faculty Committee of the Charles Phelps Taft Memorial Fund in the University of Cincinnati, who kindly extended to him the invitation to give the lectures and who generously supplied funds for the publication of this volume. At the same university the author also wishes to thank Professor Hilmar C. Krueger, who has read the manuscript in its entirety and has given helpful suggestions for its improvement. To Professor Robert L. Reynolds of the University of Wisconsin the author is similarly indebted for valuable suggestions and criticism in regard to the first, second, third, and fifth chapters and their translation. The first two chapters were also very much improved by the criticism of Professor Philip Grierson of the University of Cambridge and Professor Robert S. Lopez of Yale University. About questions presented in the fourth chapter the author profited much from discussions with Professor Fritz Machlup of the Johns Hopkins University and with Mr. Ralph Turvey of the London School of Economics. Help on numismatic problems was given by Mr. G. Bertelè of Verona and by Mr. L. Cremaschi of Pavia. To all of them the author wishes to express his gratitude. He also remembers the kindliness of the li-

ix

brary staffs at the Universities of Cincinnati and Wisconsin, at Yale University, and at the New York Public Library. The author wishes to thank Longmans, Green, and Company for their permission to quote the passage from W. Beveridge, *Prices and Wages in England from the Twelfth to the Nineteenth Century* (London, 1939), reproduced on page 52.

The author's visit to the United States was made possible by the Committee on International Exchange of Persons, which offered him a Fulbright grant. To the members of that committee and to the many friends who spoke on his behalf the author is very thankful.

*Cincinnati, November 1953*

# CONTENTS

## ILLUSTRATIONS

All illustrations follow page 12

# Money, Prices, and Civilization in the Mediterranean World

*FIFTH TO SEVENTEENTH CENTURY*

# CHAPTER I

# PRIMITIVE MONEY IN PRIMITIVE EUROPE

IF in the early Middle Ages there had existed "economists" in the Byzantine Empire, and if they had possessed the involved and technical vocabulary we have now created, those "economists," looking over their western borders at the contemporary European kingdoms, would have certainly stated that Mediterranean Europe and other parts of Western Europe were "a backward, underdeveloped area, hampered by political struggles and by lack of security, depressed by an abnormally low level of investment." As a matter of fact, since the beginning of the fifth century Mediterranean Europe, like the rest of Western Europe, had fallen into a stage of economic life near that of primitive societies, still retaining some vestiges, often more formal than substantial, of the great period of Roman imperial civilization. What happened to money in that primitive or near-primitive society?

Every student of early medieval documents is struck by the high frequency of obligations fixed and settled in kind (grain, eggs, wine, cloths, spices) or in labor. If one looks carefully at these cases, one quickly perceives that they generally refer to "unilateral payments," i.e. mainly to revenues paid by peasants or other sorts of dependents to their lords.[1] This does not mean that beyond this sector the practice was unknown; but it appears to have been used less frequently.

A second type of payments which in those centuries gained more and more in importance and diffusion was the

---

[1] H. Van Werveke, "Économie nature et économie argent," *Annales d'histoire économique et sociale*, 3 (1931), p. 428, pointed out that a careful distinction must be made between revenues and exchanges in studying the system of payments of that period.

optional system. Many documents prove that in numerous cases a debt was stipulated in a given amount of coins (I do not use the word "money," for reasons which we will see later) and at the same time in an equivalent amount of a commodity; in most cases the amount and/or nature and quality of the commodity were indicated. The debt could be settled either with the coins or with the chosen commodity.[2]

A large number of the documents that testify to this practice are again documents relating to the revenues due from peasants to their landlords, i.e. unilateral payments. But it is important to point out that a mass of other documents prove that the practice was widespread even beyond the landed estates and surely was not limited to unilateral payments only, but was common in agreements relating to all types of transactions. It would take too long to quote here even a small fraction of the numerous documents that prove this assertion. Let me give only one example that seems to me indicative. The medieval statutes of a North Italian town, reflecting a much older tradition, state that anybody going to a barber had to give him for a shave either 1 silver penny or a *sextarius* of grain.[3] Even for a small and everyday transaction the optional system was adopted.

We have first considered obligations which were fixed and settled in a certain commodity, then the sort of payments which were fixed in an optional way, in coins or in commodities. Now we can consider the third case, debts which were fixed only and explicitly in an amount of coins. We can find many documents fitting this case; but it is necessary to be careful, for they are very treacherous. I would not take their number (which *is* great) as proof of

[2] See for all this A. Dopsch, *Naturalwirtschaft und Geldwirtschaft in der Weltgeschichte* (Vienna, 1930), pp. 136ff., and M. Bloch, "Économie nature ou économie argent," *Annales d'histoire sociale*, 1 (1939), pp. 7-16.

[3] *Codex Statutorum Magnifice Communitatis atque Diocesis Alexandrinae* (Alessandria, 1547), p. 315: "Quilibet homo debeat dare barberio sextarium unum frumenti pro suo feudo vel denarium unum terdonense pro qualibet vice quod aliquem raderet et plus si ei dare placuerit."

the relative diffusion of coin payments in the economy of those centuries. In many instances where the debt was stipulated only and explicitly in an amount of, let us say, *solidi* (shillings), it was tacitly assumed that the payment could be settled with any other commodity of an equivalent value.[4] A debt stipulated in 20 *solidi* in a French document of November 1107 was, we know from a later document, settled with a horse.[5] In Spain in 905 a debt of 25 *solidi* was settled with cloth, oxen, and silver. In Spain, again, in 962 a debt of 4 *solidi* was actually paid with cloths, food, and drink, and in 933 a debt of 600 *solidi* was paid with vases, caparisons, horses, fine cloths, and coins. Most frequently in Spain debts stipulated in *solidi* were settled with grain or ewes, and the practice was so diffused that in course of time it was commonly understood that *solidus* was synonymous with one *modius of grain* or one *ewe* and the equivalence of these things was commonly and generally accepted.[6]

The examples I have quoted, and many others that could be easily assembled,[7] undoubtedly prove that under the pressure of forces that we will analyze later there materialized in daily life that distinction that we today perceive only when we read the textbooks of economics, the basic distinction between "standard of value" and "means of exchange." What was used in fixing a debt was not necessarily what was used to settle it.

The "means of exchange" were coins sometimes, but more often other commodities, of any description: foods, spices, cloth, jewelry, animals: *merce placibile*, as one document

---

[4] Other examples can be found in H. Van Werveke, "Monnaie, lingots ou marchandises," *Annales d'histoire économique et sociale*, 4 (1932), pp. 462-463. The formulae used for the settlement of debts also are very indicative. See for instance the phrase *et precium recepi a te valente solidos viginti*, quoted by C. D. F. Du Cange, *Glossarium mediae et infimae Latinitatis* (10 vols., Niort, 1883), *s.v. solidi franci.*

[5] Bloch, "Économie nature," p. 13, and Bloch, *Esquisse d'une histoire monétaire de l'Europe* (Paris, 1954), p. 31.

[6] C. Sánchez-Albornoz, "La primitiva organización monetaria de León y Castilla," *Anuario de historia del Derecho Español*, 5 (1928), p. 311, and Sánchez-Albornoz, *Estampas de la vida en León durante el siglo X* (Madrid, 1926), p. 29.

[7] See Bloch, *Esquisse d'une histoire monétaire de l'Europe*, pp. 29-33.

states.[8] The general impression is that any commodity was considered a potential means of exchange, and coins were considered just like any other commodity, one among hundreds of possible means of exchange, sometimes particularly desired and sometimes not.[9] Often preferred were peculiar types of "primitive money" like pieces of bread of standard weight.[10] Only for international transactions were coins perhaps still preferred as means of exchange to any other commodity. Actually when a merchant arrived from far away, it was more difficult to arrange business on a barter basis.[11]

As to the "standard of value" in use, it is true in the majority of the documents debts were expressed in *solidi, denarii, mancusi,* or similar terms, occasionally with the expressed option for a commodity (or labor). *Solidi, denarii,* and *mancusi* are known to be names of coins which actually existed.[12] On this ground a great French historian came to the conclusion that in the European society of the Dark Ages "la monnaie n'a pratiquement jamais cessé de tenir le rôle d'étalon des valeurs."[13] Very broadly speaking I believe that this is true. But the statement needs some qualifications. An Italian document of the eighth century, for instance, states: "pretium equorum XI pro solidis sexaginta et auri cocti pensantis solidos CCCXL. . . ."[14]

8 Du Cange, *Glossarium, s.v. solidata.*

9 Such propensity to consider any commodity as a means of exchange can explain phenomena like those of the *scutella de cambio* and *panis de cambio* studied by G. P. Bognetti, "Il problema monetario dell'economia Longobarda e il panis e la scutella de cambio," *Archivio storico Lombardo,* new series, 9 (1944), pp. 112-120.

10 See preceding note.

11 This can explain the disproportion that in some periods, mainly before the eighth century, existed between the amount of gold coins that were struck and the unimportant amount of small denominations. For all this see P. Grierson, "Problemi monetari dell'Alto Medioevo," *Bollettino della Società Pavese di Storia Patria,* 54 (1954), pp. 67-81.

12 The term *solidus* originally did indicate a gold coin (usually the Byzantine *nomisma*). After the eighth century the term was also used to mean twelve *denarii.* See chapter 4.

13 Bloch, "Économie nature," p. 14. Also see his *La société féodale* (Paris, 1939), 1, p. 107.

14 G. di Catino, *Chronicon Farfense,* edited by U. Balzani in *Fonti per la storia d'Italia,* 33 (1903), p. 150.

A document of the ninth century quoted by Du Cange says: "et pro hac donatione praedictus clericus dedit eidem Regi centum mancusas in duabus armillis et nota quod mancusas est pondus duorum solidorum et sex denariorum."[15] In both cases people used the terms *solidi* or *mancusi*, but the very notion of money underlying these terms was rather peculiar; it was the primitive notion of a standard of weight. I would not generalize too much from these and similar cases, but they seem to me indicative enough of the direction in which the system of payments was moving.[16] This vagueness in the notion of money when it was used as a standard of value was another step from the stage of "monetary" economy in the direction of a "barter" economy.

The shifting of the payment system in the direction of a barter economy seems to have been the product of different factors. I cannot pretend to list all the factors that came into the game; I very much doubt if I know all of them, but I can try to point out some of those that seem to me to have been the most effective.

If in the area of "unilateral payments"—broadly speaking, the area of revenues due to landlords—we find a great diffusion of payments stipulated and settled in kind or in labor, this fact in itself does not necessarily mean that there was no money or that the monetary system had collapsed; it can mean simply that it was more suitable to the landlords to get their tributes in kind or in labor, just as in fourteenth century England the king preferred to get some taxes in woolens or just as in modern America some local communities prefer to get labor instead of money when they collect taxes for road repairs.

If in the area of "unilateral payments" we so often see the optional system adopted, this fact may only prove that the landlords used their strong bargaining power in arranging to have, when they wanted it, plenty either of a given commodity or of the labor desired at the moment of taking pay-

---

[15] Du Cange, *Glossarium*, s.v. *mancusa*.

[16] Other cases are quoted by U. Monneret de Villard, "La monetazione nell'Italia Barbarica," *Rivista Italiana di Numismatica*, ser. 2, 2 (1919), p. 94.

ments from their dependents. An example of such a case, although very much later, I found in the accounts of a little village in the Po Valley: each of the dependents was expected to work "three days each year in the service of the seigneur or to pay him the money equivalent to the wage of three days' work." In the year of grace 1588 the seigneur "wanted the money because he did not have anything in which the labor could be used."[17]

Therefore, in the area of "revenues," payments in nature and optional payments could be the logical consequence of a particular social structure and of a strong bargaining power on the side of the landlords. But it seems also that other forces were pushing in the same direction.

In an Italian document of the eighth century, Audipertus promises to the church of St. Peter to give each year "tremisse auro aut oleo, cira, quem habuero." In another document of the same century, Guinifredus and his sons promise to give each year to the church of St. Peter "in valliente tremisse olleo, cera, auro: di ista tris res una quale habuerit."[18] In 836 we can see that a dependent of the monastery of St. Gall is expected to give each year "3 maldros sive 6 denarios vel precium 6 denariorum in ferramentis qualecumque ex his tribus facilius inveniri possimus."[19]

In these cases there is neither a question of strong bargaining power on the side of landlord nor a question of the suitability to him of getting one thing or another. Phrases like *quem habuero* or *quaecumque facilius inveniri possimus* clearly indicate another set of factors that were at work to break down the monetary system, not only in the limited area of the unilateral payments, but throughout the entire economy.

For a clearer analysis of these other factors I think it is better to look at the question from the point of view of the

[17] See C. M. Cipolla, "Finanze di borghi e castelli sotto il dominio Spagnuolo," *Bollettino storico Pavese*, 8 (1945), pp. 9, 13.

[18] *Codice diplomatico Longobardo*, edited by L. Schiaparelli in *Fonti per la storia d'Italia*, 63 (1933), pp. 219, 358.

[19] Dopsch, *Naturalwirtschaft*, p. 138.

supply of and the demand for coins. Incidentally, I am using the expressions "supply of coins" and "demand for coins" instead of "supply of money" and "demand for money" because we have already seen that for the European of that time coins were in many respects no more money than any other commodity.

Let us, therefore, consider the *supply of coins*. Many. good historians have told us of the shortage of coins in Europe in the Dark Ages. Coins were scarce; and they were scarce partly because the supply of precious metals was scarce and partly because a tremendous and widespread propensity to hoard drained relatively large amounts of the existing metals from the current supply. In addition, slow and infrequent communications and the autarchic tendencies reduced the velocity of circulation of coins. Conclusion: a general shortage. This is the over-all picture we are accustomed to. And surely there is nothing wrong in it. But there are also other elements to take into account, elements that are generally overlooked. First of all, we must consider local conditions. If communications were difficult, if the general market did not work efficiently and smoothly, it is likely that at any particular time local conditions were very diverse—that there were plenty of coins in one village or castle or town, and a shortage of coins in another village or castle or town. And these local supply conditions could be very inelastic indeed.

Secondly, one must not forget the impact of a very unbalanced distribution of income. In a given social community the economic situation of the landlord was surely not the same as that of the peasants. We cannot infer, as some historians have done, that when a landlord had his vaults full of gold and silver coins, his peasants also had plenty of coins for their daily transactions. A very unbalanced distribution of income, one has to remember, is a great handicap to the smooth working of a monetary system.

If we keep in mind these points, we can easily understand that social groups in different areas at different times could be suffering badly from a drastic local shortage of a particular type of coins or even of all types.[20]

Let us turn now to the *demand for coins*. We have already noted the great diffusion of unilateral payments settled in kind. This fact had a contractive effect on the demand for coins. This was because all the landlords who got grain, eggs, chickens, and so on from their dependents did not "demand" the coins they would probably have "demanded" if they had had to buy those commodities.

In the labor system, too, money occupied a place of minor importance. The great mass of workers did not receive wages, being paid by concessions of land tenures.

It is also obvious that in the long run the demand for money has a positive correlation with the stage of economic development and the degree of division of labor reached by any given society. The Western societies of the Dark Ages were undoubtedly at a primitive stage of economic development and if in them a division of labor existed this was certainly on a rather low level. A good part of the goods were produced by their consumers; many other goods were exchanged on a barter basis among neighbors. Such conditions further and decisively lowered the demand for coins.

Moreover, if it is true that a smoothly operating and efficient market needs a sound monetary system, it is also true that a monetary system cannot exist and cannot work if it is not supported by an efficient market. In the Europe of the early Middle Ages the market did not work either

[20] The documents offer us proofs of what I am suggesting here. An Italian document of the eighth century says: "in festivitate S. Zenonis annis singulis aut mancusos viginti aut quinquaginta solidos argenti accipere debeat a monachis Pontifex ipsius civitatis." Here again, and in other cases like this, there is no question of bargaining power, no question of gains or suitability in having this or that; it is evident here that the option between two kinds of coins, which is a particular sort of option, was adopted because the parties were foreseeing the possibility that it might be very difficult to find on the market at the moment of the payment either gold coins or, alternatively, silver ones.

F. Ughelli, *Italia sacra*, 5 (Venice, 1720), col. 706. See also L. A. Muratori, *Antiquitates Italicae Medii Aevii*, 2 (Milan, 1739), diss. 28, col. 800. Another example is quoted by M. Bloch, "Le problème de l'or au moyen âge," *Annals d'histoire économique et sociale*, 5 (1933), p. 15, n. 1, 3, 5.

very smoothly or very efficiently; this is beyond any doubt. Therefore people could not rely confidently on the market's having what they wanted. When the commodities needed are not easily or always available, the usefulness of money is greatly reduced. And consequently people prefer barter and the demand for money falls. I saw cases of this in Italy during the war. Under the massive Allied bombing, communications became difficult and supplies of food scarce and unreliable. In such a situation, my father, for instance, who owned a transportation business, when he did freighting for some producer of butter or meat often asked to be paid in butter or in meat rather than in money. Conditions not very much different must have prevailed in the Dark Ages.[21] While the transaction demand for coins was very much depressed, the demand for coins as assets to be hoarded was exceedingly high. This sort of demand, though, had rather disruptive effects on the working of the monetary system; it subtracted continuously coins from business circulation for unreasonable lengths of time and tended to shift them into the class of jewelry.

These circumstances were further aggravated by the fact that the state in the early Middle Ages did not possess the power to insist on the acceptance of its coins as legal tender, and often probably did not even wish to do so. This was certainly true of the Merovingian Franks, under whom the minting of coins was essentially a private and not a public activity, and the state did not accept coin in payment of taxes until it had been melted down and its fineness ascertained; in other words, until it had been transformed into bullion. Under the Carolingians there was sporadic legislation making it a punishable offence to refuse to accept the royal coinage, but this seems to have arisen out of the special circumstances following Charlemagne's annexation of Saxony and Bavaria, for both these regions had formerly

[21] According to some capitularia, people refused to accept and use certain types of coins because of their unreliability in respect to their fineness and weight; *Monumenta Germaniae Historica, Legum*, sectio II, *Capitularia* I, p. 74, and II, p. 302. See also Dopsch, *Naturalwirtschaft*, pp. 134f.

possessed no regular coinage of their own and it was part of the King's policy to bring them into line with the rest of his dominions. Apart from this, evidence and probability alike suggest that no serious attempt was ever made to insist on money payments.

It is time now to sum up. The list I have presented of factors operating to break down the monetary system is probably not complete at all; still I think it points out the basic and more important of the factors at work.

When a large part of the transactions are in the form of unilateral payments, when the society is at a rather primitive stage of economic development with slight division of labor, when shortages of commodities are frequent and dangerous, when because of the bad conditions of the market and an unbalanced distribution of income there are drastic and frequent shortages of coins, when, in a word, coins are not always available and not always desired, a society understandably moves toward a barter economy. The European society of the Dark Ages approached very near to this stage; it arrived at a point where coins were considered, from the point of view of means of exchange, no more money than any other commodity; in other words, where any commodity was considered also a good means of exchange. Preference seems to have been given to coins only in the area of international transactions. As standards of value also, monetary terms began to be confused with weights. The pure stage of natural economy was near indeed. But it was never reached, at least in the general picture. The force of tradition proved to be too strong. And after the second half of the tenth century the great revolution began the reversal of the trend. The splendid recovery of Western Europe that began at that time had one direction, a direction toward the triumph of money.

1. From top to bottom: An Arab *dinar* of A.H. 105. A *solidus* of Constantine VII (913-959), one of the group called *soteriki* in Italian sources from the image of the Saviour on the reverse. A *fiorino* of the earliest period, 1252-1303, before the coins were marked by the magistrates. A *ducato* of Tommaso Mocenigo, 1414-1423. (CHAPTER II.)

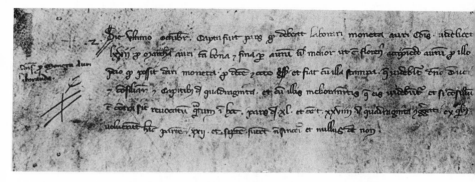

2. The decision of the Maggior Consiglio of Venice, 31 October 1284, to start t
coinage of the gold *ducato*. (CHAPTER II.)

1284, die ultimo octubris

Capta fuit pars quod debeat laborari moneta auri comunis, videlicet LXVII
marcha auri, tam bona et fina per aurum, vel melior, ut est florenus, accipiendo aurt
pro illo precio quod possit dari moneta pro decem et octo grossis; et fiat cum i
stampa que videbitur domino duci et consiliariis et capitibus de quadraginta, et c
illis melioramentis que eis videbuntur; et si consilium est contra sit revocatum quant
in hoc. Pars de XL; et erant XXVIIII de quadraginta congregati, ex quibus voluert
hanc partem XXII et septem fuerunt non sinceri et nullus de non.

(Archivio di Stato di Venezia, *Maggior Consiglio*, registro "Luna," c. 48 v., al
ottobre 1284.)

3. The *denarius* (pen-
ny) of Charlemagne.
(CHAPTER IV.)

4. Actual size of the petty
*denarius* (penny) and *grosso*
(groat) of Venice at the time
of the introduction of the groat,
under Doge Enrico Dandolo
(1192-1205). (CHAPTER IV.)

5. A page of the inventory of the library of Sylanus Niger. In the Archivio di Stato, Pavia. (CHAPTER V.)

6. The study room of a copyist of books, with the instruments of his craft. A painting on a column of the Church of San Nicolo in Treviso, fifteenth century. (CHAPTER V.)

# CHAPTER II

# THE DOLLARS OF THE
# MIDDLE AGES

LAST year I had to travel across Europe. I had my wallet full of different pieces of paper, printed with different colors, in different languages, with different symbols— charming examples of the European dislike of uniformity. I also had some other pieces of paper to perform the function of reserve money. On each of them was printed the statement that the Treasury of the United States of America was ready to give *one dollar in silver payable to the bearer on demand.* These pieces of paper, I knew, were more generally acceptable than any European currency. In any part of Europe there could be no difficulty in finding people who would take them as money. I could spend them everywhere, asking for everything. They were, they are, the international currency *par excellence.*

This phenomenon of an international currency, a sort of super money, is not new in European economic history.[1] Several years ago one of the most brilliant of economic historians wrote an article on the gold *solidus* of the Byzantine Empire and entitled it "The Dollar of the Middle Ages."[2] As a matter of fact, through the centuries of the Middle Ages there were many types of "dollars." Their story seems to me interesting enough to be told at length;

[1] In the previous chapter I have shown that during the Dark Ages many transactions were often made on a barter basis, but that (1) coins did not disappear completely, and (2) coins remained the preferred means of exchange in international trade. Taking into account these two qualifications, the reader will realize that there is no contradiction between what has been written in the previous chapter and what will be said in this chapter about the circulation of the Byzantine *solidus* and the Moslem *dinar.*

[2] R. S. Lopez, "The Dollar of the Middle Ages," *Journal of Economic History,* 11 (1951), pp. 209-234. A parallel between the Byzantine *solidus* and the dollar was also traced by G. I. Bratianu, *Études byzantines d'histoire économique et sociale* (Paris, 1938), p. 237.

it can help us to discover some of the qualities and some of the behavior of an "international currency."

Before going into details I think it is important to make clear that monetary sovereignty is a very recent thing. As late as the nineteenth century no western state enjoyed a complete monetary sovereignty. The more or less faithful adherence to the strict rules of the gold standard prevented national authorities from keeping full control of monetary movements. Yet a step was then taken that was important for the achievement of monetary sovereignty: from the middle of the century in each state, only its own national currency circulated.

In previous centuries the situation had been very different. In every state, be it a feudal state, or a city state, or a national state, foreign coins circulated normally and widely along with local coins. Foreign coins, like local coins, were used as assets to be hoarded and as means of payment in current transactions. Normally there was nothing illegal in that.

Whenever a state organization was rising in strength and efficiency, one hears of its efforts to keep out of monetary circulation certain types of foreign coins. In the sixteenth and seventeenth century state of Milan, for instance, there was a constant effort to forbid the circulation of those foreign coins that did not maintain a stable weight or a stable fineness.[3] These provisions and these efforts did not detract from the basic tenet of monetary organization of those centuries, that foreign coins had the same rights as national coins and that they could freely come in and freely circulate without any particular limitation.

This statement, though, needs a qualification. Particularly for the second half of the Middle Ages, when we speak of coins that could freely move throughout Europe, we refer especially to the big, full-bodied coins, the so-called *moneta grossa*. Small fractional coins did not generally circulate outside the limited area where they were issued;

[3] C. M. Cipolla, *Les mouvements monétaires dans l'État de Milan, 1580-1700* (Paris, 1952), p. 14.

they served the needs of local transactions. Moreover, since these petty coins were often nothing but tokens, beyond their issuing area they were not easily accepted or always admitted. Anyway, petty coins represented the smaller part of the value of total circulation.[4] The greater part was represented by the big, full-bodied coins and all these were practically "international currencies."

If one looks more closely at the mass of the existing and circulating big coins, at their types and their characteristics, one realizes that indeed they were all more or less international currencies, but (1) that there always existed one among them that predominated as the international currency and everywhere enjoyed much more prestige, being much more eagerly demanded and much more easily accepted, and (2) that most of the other big coins in circulation and issued in the different states were nothing but a more or less faithful copy of the prevailing one, imitating its weight, its fineness, and often even the design and the inscriptions.

From the point of view of *the prevailing* international currency, the Middle Ages divided itself into three long periods: a first period from the beginning of the Middle Ages to the end of the seventh century; a second period from the beginning of the eighth century to the middle of the thirteenth; and a third period from the middle of the thirteenth century to the end of the Middle Ages.

In the first period (fifth to seventh century), throughout the Mediterranean—in the rich towns of the Near East, in the markets of North Africa, in the ports of Italy, around the monasteries and the castles of France and of Spain— one coin enjoyed an absolute prestige over the others, the gold *solidus* of the Byzantine Empire.[5] Kosmas Indicopleustes, a Greek monk, who in his youth had been an adventurous merchant and traveler, could proudly state in the

---

[4] See for instance the calculations made by Cipolla, *Les mouvements*, p. 14.

[5] The Byzantine gold *solidus* was called *nomisma* by the Greeks and *bezant* by the Westerners. In the thirteenth century it was also called *hyperperon*.

sixth century that the gold coin of the Byzantine Empire "is accepted everywhere from end to end of the earth. It is admired by all men and in all kingdoms because no kingdom has a currency that can be compared to it."[6] Numerous documents and modern archeological discoveries prove to us that Kosmas told the truth.[7] This situation lasted until the end of the seventh century; until that date we can safely say that the Mediterranean was a "*nomisma* area."

In the last decade of the seventh century that unity broke up. By that time the Arabs had been upon the scene for a long time. Yet, if they had changed the political and the religious map of the Mediterranean, they had not changed the monetary map. In the first generations they continued to use for their transactions the Byzantine gold coins (which they called *dinars*) and the Persian silver coins (which they called *dirhems*). If they struck gold coins, they simply imitated the coin of the Byzantine emperors. As an ancient Moslem writer said: "Before the reign of Abd el Malek all the dinars had Greek inscriptions."[8]

Calif Abd el Malek brought about the great innovation.[9] I cannot resist the temptation of translating an ancient Moslem account of his reform that has the flavor of the *Arabian Nights*.

I came one day, said el Kesay, to the house of Harun al Rashid and found him in a room in his palace. . . . He held in his hand a *dirhem* on which the inscription glis-

---

[6] *Cosmae aegyptii monachi christiana topographia*, edited by B. de Montfaucon (Paris, 1707), p. 148; E. O. Winstedt, *The Christian Topography of Cosmas Indicopleustes* (Cambridge, England, 1909), p. 81.

[7] See for instance the numerous documents quoted by C. D. F. Du Cange, *Glossarium mediae et infimae Latinitatis* (10 vols., Niort, 1883), *s.v. Byzantium*, and those quoted by U. Monneret de Villard, "La monetazione nell'Italia Barbarica," *Rivista Italiana di Numismatica*, ser. 2, 2 (1919), pp. 78, n. 1 and 4, and pp. 101-109.

[8] M. H. Sauvaire, "Matériaux pour servir à l'histoire de la numismatique et de la métrologie musulmanes," *Journal Asiatique*, ser. 7, 14 (1879), p. 477.

[9] Among others see E. von Bergmann, "Die Nominale der Münzreform des Chalifen Abdulmelik," *Sitzungsberichte der philosophisch-historischen Classe der Kaiserlichen Akademie der Wissenschaften*, 56 (1870), pp. 239-266.

tened; he was looking at it attentively. The Calif had entertained me often.

"Do'st thou know," he asked me, "who first instituted the custom of engraving these characters on gold and silver?"

"Sir," I answered, "it was el Malek."

"And for what reason?"

"All that I know," I replied, "is that it was he who first established that custom."

"Well, then, I will teach thee. Papyrus was made [in Egypt] for the Byzantines. Now as those who lived in Egypt were Christians of the same rite as the Emperor of the Byzantines, the papyrus they made carried a design in Greek characters, containing these words: 'Father, Son, and Holy Ghost.' This state of things continued throughout the first days of Islam, and survived without change until the reign of Abd el Malek ibn Merwan. . . . One day . . . having looked at the design, he ordered that it be translated into Arabic, which was done. Angered by such a formula . . . , he ordered that a written order be sent to Abd el Aziz ibn Merwan, who was his governor in Egypt, to suppress the use of this decoration on the cloth, papyrus, dyestuffs, etc., that were made there, and to order the laborers employed in the making of the papyrus to replace it by the formula of the recognition of Allah's unity: 'Allah is witness that there is no God but Allah.'

"Now, after the papyri had received the new design containing the formula of Allah's unity, and when the new papyri were brought into the country of the Byzantines, the news spread and finally came to the ears of their emperor. When he saw the translation of the design which was made for him, he became very angry, cursing it and heaping blasphemous terms upon it. He wrote at once to Abd el Malek saying, 'The making of papyrus in Egypt and indeed of all objects that receive a design is done for the Byzantines, and they have not ceased to use the Byzantine design until the moment when thou prohibited it. Now if the Califs, thy predecessors, have done well, thou hast

17

done ill, and if it is thou who art in the right, it is they who were in error. Choose then from these two alternatives the one which thou preferest and which pleases thee better. I send thee a present worthy of thy rank; I would desire thee to restore the ancient design—that is an act for which I will thank thee. . . .' [Abd el Malek having left three ambassadors without an answer], the Byzantine Emperor wrote again: 'I swear it by the Messiah, thou wilt give the order to restore the design as it was, or I will give orders to coin *dinars* and *dirhems*—and thou knowest that not a coin has been struck outside of my empire—and we will place insults to thy Prophet on them as inscriptions, that reading them may make the sweat start on thy forehead. . . .'

"When Abd el Malek was informed of the letter, the situation appeared serious to him, and he found himself most embarrassed. . . . And he called the Musulmans together and asked their counsel. But none of them could present a practical solution. However, Rouh ibn Zanba spoke in this manner: 'Thou knowest very well who can get thee out of thy difficulty, but thou keepest him to one side.' 'Evil come upon thee!' exclaimed el Malek. 'Who is it?' 'Command,' continued his councilor, 'that the Fount of Science of the Prophet's House come before thee.' 'Thou art right,' said Abd el Malek, 'I have not thought of him.' He wrote to his governor in Medina, saying, 'Send me Mohammed ibn Aly Ebn el Hosayn, with all the honors due to him; give him 100 thousand *dirhems* for his retinue and 300 thousand for his expenses on the road. . . .'

"At the same time he kept the Byzantine ambassador with him until the coming of Mohammed ibn Aly. As soon as ibn Aly arrived he was informed of what had happened. He told the Calif, 'Do not let this trouble thee for two reasons. First, Allah cannot permit that the threats uttered by the King of the Byzantines against the successor of Allah will come to anything; second, there is a way out of the difficulty.'

" 'And what is that?' asked Abd el Malek.

" 'Thou wilt immediately call together workers who will strike before thee the dies for *dirhems* and *dinars*, on which thou wilt inscribe the formula of the unity of Allah and the mention of the Prophet of Allah, the first on the obverse of the coins, and the second on the reverse. On the border of the coins thou wilt mention the town where the coin is struck and the year in which it is struck. . . .'

"Abd el Malek followed his advice. Mohammed ibn Aly el Hosayn also advised him to order the use of the new coins in all the towns of Islam, and to command the people to use them in their transactions under pain of death. . . . Order was given to melt down the old coins and to send them to mints to be changed into Islamic coins.

"Abd el Malek then acted thus, and sent the Byzantine ambassador back to his Emperor. . . ."

At this point Rashid threw his coin to one of his servants.[10]

Charming as it is, the story told by Harun al Rashid was somewhat incomplete. There are indications that the design on the Egyptian papyrus was not the only reason behind the monetary reform of Abd el Malek. It seems that the complete indifference of the first Moslem rulers toward monetary matters resulted in widespread disorder and private and public speculations.[11] Furthermore, because coins that circulated among Moslems and particularly the Persian silver *dirhem* were of very different weights, people began to refer to ideal standard units of account representing fixed weights of gold or silver; and it seems that Abd el Malek with his reform wanted to put into circulation real coins of value equal to these units of account.[12]

Whatever the reasons for the reform, it is beyond doubt that it marked a real turning point in the monetary history

10 Sauvaire, "Matériaux pour servir," p. 475; also J. von Karabacek, "Zur orientalischen Altertumskunde, II: die Arabischen Papyrusprotokolle," *Sitzungsberichte der philosophisch-historischen Classe der Kaiserlichen Akademie der Wissenschaften*, 161 (1909), pp. 1-103, who gives full information on the sources.

11 Sauvaire, "Matériaux pour servir" (1879), p. 478.

12 Sauvaire, "Matériaux pour servir" (1879), p. 506.

of the Mediterranean. The new Moslem coins soon enjoyed a tremendous prestige,[13] and although the *dinar* did not drive out of the Mediterranean area the Byzantine *nomisma*, it broke down the monopoly of the latter as an international currency. After the late seventh century the Mediterranean world had two strong coins that enjoyed a predominant international prestige, and both were of non-Western origin. Western Europe did not try to compete with the Byzantines or the Moslems in this matter. Economically and politically too weak, it acquiesced in a very passive role. It gave up any pretension of issuing regularly a gold coinage and basically shifted to a silver one.[14]

There were other, related developments in the course of the centuries. At the end of the twelfth century and in the first half of the thirteenth some Italian silver coins—the groats—appeared side by side with *nomismata* and *dinars* in the role of a widely accepted international currency in the Mediterranean area. They, even more than the *augustales* of Frederick II or the gold coins of Spain, foretold the succeeding revolutionary developments.

It is with the middle of the thirteenth century that the situation prevailing in the first half of the Middle Ages was dramatically reversed. In 1252 Italian merchant republics began to strike a coin of pure gold at the weight of about 3½ grams. In the very first days the newcomers found some difficulties; "e non n'era quasi chi il volesse," said an old chronicler. But the first difficulties were soon and completely overcome. From then to the end of the

[13] On the diffusion of the *dinar* see Monneret de Villard, "La monetazione nell'Italia Barbarica," pp. 73-98; for a critical view, P. Grierson, "Carolingian Europe and the Arabs: The Myth of the *Mancus*," *Revue Belge de Philologie et d'Histoire*, 32 (1954), pp. 1059-1074, and F. J. Himly, "Y a-t-il emprise musulmane sur l'économie des états Européens du VIIIe au Xe siècle?" *Revue suisse d'histoire*, 5 (1955), pp. 31-81.

[14] A regular gold coinage practically ceased in Western Europe in the eighth century and in the Italian peninsula in the second half of the same century. Even in Moslem Spain no gold was struck between the beginning of the eighth century and the beginning of the tenth. See G. C. Miles, *The Coinage of the Umayyads of Spain* (New York, 1950), p. 87. In the few cases in which a ruler wished to coin a few gold pieces that could have a wide circulation, he struck more or less faithful imitations of the Moslem *dinar* or of the Byzantine *nomisma*.

Middle Ages the dollar of the Mediterranean area was the gold coin of the Italian republics. As a matter of fact, this last period can be divided into two subperiods. Between the middle of the thirteenth century and the end of the fourteenth the gold coin of Florence enjoyed by far the greatest prestige, and the officials of the mint of Florence could proudly claim the "communem cursum quem habet dicta moneta auri per universum orbem terrarum."[15] In the fifteenth century it was the gold coin of Venice which represented the international currency *par excellence*.[16]

By the end of the Middle Ages the situation was completely the reverse of what it had been at the beginning. If then the Europeans had to use the gold coins of the Byzantine Emperor, now the case was that "el emperador feu batre moneda en manera de ducat Venecia."[17]

So far we have met the Byzantine *nomisma*, the Moslem *dinar*, the *fiorino* of Florence, and the *ducato* of Venice. We know also about the historical periods in which each one of them enjoyed a tremendous international reputation. What were the reasons behind their successive triumphant supremacies? In other words, do their different histories show some common elements so that, following the proud custom of the economists, we too may try to formulate a "general theory"?

As a matter of fact, it seems to me that these currencies showed at least three common characteristics.

First of all, they always presented a unit embodying a high value. The Byzantine *solidus* was $\frac{1}{72}$ of a Roman pound. If one accepts the equivalence of 327.45 grams for

15 I. Orsini, *Storia delle monete della Repubblica Fiorentina* (Florence, 1760), p. 1.

16 The prestige of the *ducato* in the fifteenth century is most clearly shown by the fact that the rulers in both the eastern and western Mediterranean, Moslems as well as Christians, used it as their standard when reforming their coinage. On it was based the Mamluk *ashrafti*, the Ottoman *altun*, the Portuguese *cruzado*, and the Castilian *ducato*. See H. E. Ives, *The Venetian Gold Ducat and Its Imitations* edited and annotated by P. Grierson (New York, 1954).

17 The text is quoted by E. Stein, "Untersuchungen zur spätbyzantinischen Verfassungs- und Wirtschaftsgeschichte," *Mitteilungen zur Osmanischen Geschichte*, 2 (1923-1925), p. 13, n. 1.

a Roman pound, one must admit a theoretical weight of the *solidus* of 4.55 grams.[18] If one accepts the equivalence of 322.56 grams for a Roman pound, one arrives at a theoretical weight of 4.48 grams.[19] W. Wroth, who weighed all the imperial coins in the British Museum, arrived at the conclusion that "the weight of this coin varied but little through the long period of its existence. It is always of more than 3.88 grams and the heaviest extant specimens usually weigh from 4.40 to 4.53 grams. Specimens that attain 4.53 grams are, however, decidedly uncommon."[20] We can, therefore, safely conclude that the Byzantine *solidus* represented normally around 4.5 grams of pure gold.[21]

The Moslem *dinar* did not differ very much. As a matter of fact, this coin derived from the Byzantine *solidus*. In the Umayyad East the standard weight seems to have been that of 4.25 grams; an average, perhaps, of the weights of the worn Byzantine coins that were in circulation in the Moslem territory at the time of Abd el Malek.[22] In Umayyad Spain the *dinars*, struck before the eighth century, when they ceased to be issued, were generally heavier than those in the East, the average weighing about 4.28 grams.[23] The gold coins of the Italian merchant republics were of about 3.5 grams of gold.

The dollars of the Middle Ages—the *nomisma*, *dinar*, *fiorino*, and *ducato*—were struck in pure gold and ranged in weight between 3.5 and 4.5 grams. The present-day United States dollar is equivalent to something less than

[18] This was the weight of the Roman pound according to F. C. Hultsch, *Griechische und Römische Metrologie* (Berlin, 1882), pp. 155-161.

[19] This was the weight of the Roman pound according to L. Naville, "Fragments de métrologie antique," *Revue suisse de numismatique*, 22 (1920), pp. 42-60, and Naville, "La livre romaine et le denier de la loi salique," *Revue suisse de numismatique*, 22 (1920) pp. 257-263.

[20] W. Wroth, *Catalogue of the Imperial Byzantine Coins in the British Museum* (London, 1908), I, p. lxxiv.

[21] Preserved monetary weights of that period clearly confirm the weight of about 4.5 grams. See the bibliography quoted in D. A. Zakythinos, *Crise monétaire et crise économique à Byzance du XIII au XV siècle* (Athens, 1948), p. 3.

[22] Sauvaire, "Matériaux pour servir" (1869), pp. 479, 487, 506.

[23] Miles, *The Coinage of the Umayyads of Spain*, p. 90.

1 gram. But a precise comparison has also to take into account that the purchasing power of gold in terms of other commodities was generally much higher in the Middle Ages than it is today.

A second important factor upholding the prestige of the coins we are discussing seems to have been their remarkable intrinsic stability for a long time following their first issue.[24] The weight and the fineness of the Byzantine *solidus* remained fundamentally stable in the first five centuries of the Middle Ages. Only with the eleventh century did it begin to be seriously and progressively debased.[25]

If we turn to the Moslem *dinar*, we can easily see that it too maintained intrinsic stability in the first two centuries of its existence. This is true for the *dinars* struck in the East. It also seems to be true for the *dinars* struck in Spain.[26] It was only in the eleventh century that the Spanish *dinar* began to be seriously debased.

The *fiorino* of Florence remained a very stable coin for a century and a half after its first issue. When in the fourteenth century France was in the throes of monetary troubles, the chronicler Giovanni Villani could proudly set against the unstable French coins "il nostro fiorino ch'é ferma e legal moneta di fino oro."[27] The *fiorino* suffered some troubles at the beginning of the fifteenth century. In Florence were issued some types of florin with a lighter weight, and abroad imitations of the florin were issued at a lighter weight.[28] It may be that these misadventures played some part in the replacement of the *fiorino* by the Venetian *ducato* as the dollar of the last part of the Middle Ages. As a matter of fact, the Venetian *ducato*, which was

[24] By intrinsic stability is meant stability in the weight and alloy of the coin. It does not necessarily mean stability in terms of other commodities.

[25] See for all this P. Grierson, "The Debasement of the Bezant in the Eleventh Century," *Byzantinische Zeitschrift*, 47 (1954), pp. 379-394.

[26] Miles, *The Coinage of the Umayyads of Spain*, p. 90.

[27] G. Villani, *Cronica* (Florence, 1823), lib. XI, ch. 72. In the edition of Milan, 1803 (Classici Italiani), the passage is found in chapter 71.

[28] See A. Nagl, "Die Goldwährung und die handelsmässige Geldrechnung im Mittelalter," *Numismatische Zeitschirft*, 26 (1895), pp. 98-101.

first coined in 1284, kept both its weight and fineness re-markably intact up to the end of the Venetian Republic.

High unitary value and intrinsic stability, necessary con-ditions as they may have been, were certainly not sufficient to guarantee to the coins the international success they had. One does not need to go beyond the centuries we are consid-ering to find proofs of this. The gold coin of the Emperor Frederick II, that of "messire saint Louis," and that of Henry III of England were certainly good pieces, but they never had the role of the *nomisma*, the *dinar*, the *fiorino*, and the *ducato*. To be a "dollar" a currency must be backed by a sound and strong economy which participates exten-sively in international trade.

The triumph of the *nomisma* would have been com-pletely inconceivable without the industrial and commercial power of the Byzantine Empire in the first part of the Middle Ages. The basic reason for the success of the re-form of Abd el Malek and the wide circulation of his coins throughout the world was, with due respect for Allah, the economic significance of the new Moslem empire and its great role in the system of international exchange of those generations. If one wants to understand the reasons for the triumph of the *fiorino* of Florence in the second half of the thirteenth century and in part of the fourteenth, one must keep in mind the tremendous expanding force of the Flor-entine economy at that time and its great impact on inter-national banking and trade. In the same way, the triumph of the *ducato* would remain incomprehensible if it could not be related to the expansion of the Venetian economy and the role of that city in the system of international transac-tions during the fifteenth century. High unitary value, in-trinsic stability, support by an economy at the same time strong, sound, and playing a preeminent role in the system of international exchanges—these seem to have been the three basic elements of the formula that made the fortunes of the "dollars of the Middle Ages."[29]

[29] The three factors discussed in the text probably were the most important in making the fortune of the medieval "dollar." But certainly

The importance of each of these elements was certainly not the same. We have no test for an objective measurement and any consideration must rest on personal judgment. My personal feeling is that in the cases which I have presented, of the three elements—high unitary value, intrinsic stability, and economic background—the last has always been the most significant. I am certainly convinced of the high importance of intrinsic stability, but I believe that we must not look at the question with too modern an eye.[30] I think it is necessary to distinguish between stability in fineness and stability in weight. In the habit of the Middle Ages of using coins by weight rather than by tale, it was especially the stability in fineness that mattered. The maintenance of stable fineness was very important for the destiny of a coin and this importance was in direct correlation to the difficulty of ascertaining the fineness at the moment of payment.

The importance of the high unitary value, which was not as great as that of the other two elements, was based on logical and emotional factors. It is easily understood that a low unitary value would not add prestige and would confine a coin to the limited area of local transactions. The high unitary value of the dollars of the Middle Ages was important not only for the prestige it gave, but also for the

other factors existed. The fact that a coin maintained an unvarying type would greatly advance its popularity, particularly among illiterate populations. In other cases superstition or religion could exert an important influence. It seems, for instance, that the popularity of the Venetian gold *ducato* among the Christian population of the Levant was caused to a large extent by the fact that that population believed the effigy of San Marco and of the doge to be that of Constantine the Great and his mother, Helen. Cf. F. W. Hasluck, "Constantinate," in *Essays and Studies Presented to W. Ridgeway* (Cambridge, England, 1913), pp. 635-637. Similarly, today, in Abyssinia the popularity of the Maria Theresa *thaler* is partly due to the fact that the Abyssinian Coptic Christians believe this effigy to be that of the Virgin. Cf. L. M. Nesbitt, *Desert and Forest* (Bristol, 1955), p. 16. On the "dollars" of the period after the Middle Ages, see A. Dieudonné, "Des especes de circulation internationale en Europe depuis Saint Louis," *Revue suisse de numismatique*, 22 (1920), pp. 3-39.

30 Again I wish to emphasize that intrinsic stability (which means stability in terms of that metal of which the coin is composed) does not necessarily mean stability in terms of other commodities. Yet the former is at least one form of stability.

social implications it brought into play. Since the mass of people possessed low purchasing power, the high unitary value made the dollars of the Middle Ages "aristocratic coins" in the sense that they circulated only among the upper classes and only in special sectors of economic life.[31] The fact that in the stratified society different classes use different types of money presents a great problem with many consequences, to some of which I will refer in the following chapter.

[31] The fact was noted by Bloch, "Le problème de l'or," and then emphasized by A. Sapori in one of his well-known studies, *Studi di storia economica medievale* (Florence, 1946), p. 671, n. 1.

# CHAPTER III

# THE BIG PROBLEM OF THE PETTY COINS

EVERY elementary textbook of economics gives the standard formula for maintaining a sound system of fractional money: to issue on government account small coins having a commodity value lower than their monetary value; to limit the quantity of these small coins in circulation; to provide convertibility with unit money. One can also add the rule that fractional money cannot be legal tender in payments over a certain amount, although some economists do not hold this last ingredient to be essential to the recipe.[1]

Simple as this formula may seem, it took centuries to work it out. In England it was not applied until 1816, and in the United States it was not accepted before 1853. Its application has been most important for the successful functioning of modern monetary systems.[2]

No society which uses both gold and silver for coinage purposes can maintain a satisfactory and stable monetary system if it mints petty coins with a metallic content equal to their circulation value. In any such case in effect, the continuous fluctuations in the market prices of gold, silver, and copper cause one or the other of two effects: they oblige the authorities to change continually the legal ratios of the coinages and the rates of exchange between the big coins and the petty coins; or they cause one of the two sorts of money to disappear from circulation.

[1] See E. Cannan, *Money* (Westminster, 1929), pp. 31f. On the views of the early monetary theoreticians see A. E. Monroe, *Monetary Theory before Adam Smith* (Cambridge, Mass., 1923) p. 96.

[2] One modern economist has pointed out, "It is probably not too much to say that this discovery made possible the rise of the international gold standard by demonstrating that a satisfactory system of subsidiary currency was possible without depending upon either a silver or a bimetallic standard." See A. E. Whittlesey, *Principles and Practices of Money and Banking* (New York, 1948), p. 198.

To this great inconvenience there was in the Middle Ages added another. In most cases the mints were not operated directly by the state, but were farmed out to private persons who coined money out of 'the metal that other private persons brought to them. The controlling interest of these mint farmers was naturally that of private profit, not that of public utility. In those cases in which a king himself ran a mint he also acted more often as a private entrepreneur than as head of the state. Profits to the moneyers were high on the gold and good silver coinage, but were low on the coinage of petty coins unless there was a chance of gain through speculation upon the difference between their face value and their commodity value. Whenever the monetary authorities tried to require a metallic content equal or nearly equal in value to face value, the issue of petty coins diminished drastically and the society began to suffer a shortage of money of this type.

Until recently many persons failed to understand the true nature and origin of those monetary disorders, continuing wrongly to maintain that a money system would be sound and would function only when the intrinsic value of the petty coins was maintained at par with their nominal value. This erroneous view dominated a good part of the monetary history of the medieval and early modern centuries. However, though this was one of the leitmotifs of monetary theory, it did not follow that monetary practice in those days was always inspired by it or remained faithful to its principles. Frequently, on the contrary, to overcome budgetary problems or for other economic, political, or social reasons, both medieval and modern administrations debased their petty coins, trying to make them circulate at a nominal value higher than their metallic value.

Nevertheless, maneuvers of this sort were, in the Middle Ages as in early modern times, generally considered to be dishonest expedients, low political or fiscal tricks. Only in the sixteenth and seventeenth centuries did some monetary experts begin to abandon the traditional point of view. In other words, some thinkers began to assert not only that it was possible to make petty coins circulate as token money,[3] but that it was necessary to do so if a sound monetary system was to be maintained. One of the most brilliant expositions of this concept is that of Geminiano Montanari, a professor of mathematics at the University of Padua, in a book upon monetary policy which he wrote in the second half of the seventeenth century. "It is clear enough," he wrote, "that it is not necessary for a prince to strike petty coins having a metallic content equal to their face value, provided he does not strike more of them than is sufficient for the use of his people, sooner striking too few than striking too many. If the prince strikes only as many as the people need, he may strike [petty coins] of whatever metallic content he wishes. . . ." To this he added, "I am afraid this may seem a paradox to some persons but I think that should the prince refrain from gaining anything from petty coins and strike them of a metallic content equal to the face value minus the cost of striking, this may some day provoke some trouble in the field of larger coins."[4]

Ideas of this sort certainly were not universally accepted in the seventeenth or even in the eighteenth century,[5] but they were spreading.

The discovery that it was better to use token coins for small denominations did not actually solve the problem. As Geminiano Montanari clearly wrote, and as other economists and statesmen affirmed, token money could indeed be used provided the quantity of it in circulation was regulated.

[3] I will call *token money* the money "whose value is materially greater than the value of the stuff of which it is composed," and *full-bodied money* the money "whose value is not materially greater than that of its component stuff." For these definitions see D. H. Robertson, *Money* (Cambridge, England, 1948), p. 47.

[4] G. Montanari, *La zecca in consulta di stato*, in A. Graziani, *Economisti del Cinque e del Seicento* (Bari, 1913), pp. 290-294.

[5] For instance, in the seventeenth century the monetary legislation of Piedmont and Savoy was still dominated by the confusion between commodity money and fiduciary money. See G. Praj, "La moneta Piemontese ai tempi di Vittorio Amedeo I e Carlo Emanuele II," *Bollettino storico-bibliografico Subalpino*, 40 (1938), p. 246. And many of the eighteenth century economists were still not inclined to take the risks involved in the issuance of fiduciary subsidiary coins. See Monroe, *Monetary Theory*, pp. 189f.

The "quantity" had to be regulated. But how? G. A. Thesauro, in a treatise on money printed in Turin in 1607, advised, "The quantity [of petty money] should be limited in such a way that it is scarcely sufficient for people to make their petty purchases and to take care of fractional payments," and he strengthened this view, stating, "it is good to restrict the issues of petty coins because these coins must be struck only for the petty purchases of food and for functions subsidiary to those of (*pro supplemento*) the bigger coins."[6] In 1613 A. Serra wrote that petty coins ought to be restricted "to those quantities which are sufficient for making change."[7] Some time later a Piedmontese senator wrote that "the sure way" to maintain a stable and sound monetary system was "not to strike more petty coins than are needed for petty business."[8] Geminiano Montanari, we have seen, still later asserted it was necessary for a prince not to "strike more [petty coins] than [are] sufficient for the use of his people, sooner striking too few than striking too many."[9] Again, in the eighteenth century, another Italian economist, G. B. Vasco, expressed the same concept when he asserted that "the quantity of small coins has to be proportioned to meet only the needs of daily petty business."[10] The monetary laws of Piedmont in 1755, moreover, were intended "to do away with the quantity of fractional money exceeding the needs of the petty trade for which it is intended."[11]

All of these statements were right. But they did not help very much. What exactly were those "needs of petty trade"?

[6] G. A. Thesauro, *Tractatus novus de augmento ac variatione monetarum* (Turin, 1607), pp. 27, 33. On page 33 the author also clearly states that "quando nimis erose monete cuditur vel aliunde importatur tunc sempre alteratur pretium perfectioris monete."

[7] A. Serra, *Breve trattato delle cause che possono fare abbondare li regni di oro e argento*, in Graziani, *Economisti*, p. 217.

[8] Praj, "La moneta Piemontese," p. 235.

[9] Montanari, *La zecca in consulta di stato*, p. 290.

[10] G. B. Vasco, *Osservazioni* in *Scrittori Classici Italiani di Economia Politica, parte moderna*, edited by A. Custodi (Milan, 1804), 35, pp. 335, 341.

[11] *Raccolta delle leggi della R. Casa di Savoia*, edited by F. A. Duboin (Turin, 1851), t. 18, vol. 20, p. 1330.

How measure them? Here lay a real difficulty. In Spain the mints were required to issue stated proportions of coins of the various denominations.[12] In seventeenth century Venice the issue of petty coins was limited to stated quantities. In Rome under Pope Innocent X (1644-1655) the monetary officials of the Papal States decided that no more than 200 *scudi* worth of petty coins had to be minted in any one year.[13] Stated proportions or stated quantities were the result of a rough guess, and, besides, guesses of this sort did not take into account the fact that a given "quantity" or a given "proportion" of small coins may be too small in one year and too large in another.

What both theorists and practical men of the time failed to discover was the fact that the quantity of petty coins in circulation would become automatically regulated if the state did two things: assume the monopoly of the coinage of token pieces and guarantee their convertibility with big, full-bodied coins.[14]

In judging the failure of the monetary authorities of the time to adopt the policy of convertibility we need to note that an obstacle to the adoption of that principle existed in a circumstance beyond the desires of the governments—namely, their limited sovereignty in monetary matters. All too generally, into and inside the boundaries of a state, there flowed and circulated masses of petty coins from all the neighboring states. More than once governments of the time tried and failed to dry up such tidal floods. It is evident that under such circumstances the monetary authorities found it impossible to guarantee convertibility.

Mediterranean Europe failed to discover a good and automatic device to control the quantity of petty coins to be left in circulation. Eventually it also failed to maintain a

[12] A. P. Usher, *The Early History of Deposit Banking in Mediterranean Europe* (Cambridge, Mass., 1943), p. 198.

[13] Montanari, *La zecca in consulta di stato*, p. 353.

[14] In the general failure, a remarkable exception which represents a pioneer experiment of controlling "quantity" also through "convertibility" is the privilege accorded by the Spanish King to the town of Barcelona in 1481. On this case see Usher, *The Early History of Deposit Banking*, p. 232.

stable metallic content in its small denominations, at least in the long run. I cannot enter now into the long discussion about the ultimate causes of this second failure; a discussion which is much more complicated than many historians and many economists have suspected. What I want to point out are some general patterns of the movements of petty money in the theoretical and institutional environment of those centuries.

When a debasement was put into effect, the maneuver gave to the mint farmers (or in some cases to the king or to the private citizen, according to the institutional regulation of the mint) a good chance of gain through speculation upon the difference between the current face value of the petty coins and their newly debased metallic content. Consequently the issues of petty coins entered a period of boom. Quite generally the quantity of petty coins in circulation quickly reached a point at which their current value was forced down till it reached the commodity value of the coins. At this point nobody had an interest in striking petty coins. Issues contracted until a new debasement was decreed.

This particular system was not born of any theoretical pattern. It was the empirical result of the automatic play of forces of adaptation and of reaction. By its very nature, it was not a device that would operate smoothly, but it was a device that created a chain of alternate periods of shortages of petty coins and excessive coining.[15]

The progressive debasement of the petty coins and the failure to control their quantity eventually caused a progressive rise of the market rate at which the stable gold coins were circulating.[16] In Florence, for instance, the great

[15] This oscillatory movement is clearly perceived when one observes the fluctuations of the rates of exchange between the petty coins and the big, full-bodied coins all through the Middle Ages. See C. M. Cipolla, *Studi di storia della moneta: I movimenti dei cambi in Italia dal sec. XIII al XV* (Pavia, 1948), pp. 98-105.

[16] I think it is important to recall that the two phenomena—debasement of petty coins and rise of the rates of exchange—even though they had a close correlation in the long run, did not usually have a close correlation in the short run. See C. M. Cipolla, *Les mouvements monétaires dans l'État de Milan, 1580-1700* (Paris, 1952), pp. 19f.

industrial center of the Middle Ages, it took only 20 shillings of petty money to acquire a golden florin in 1252. By the beginning of the eighteenth century it took 266 shillings.[17] In the long run the rise of these rates of exchange was indicative of the debasement undergone by the petty coins.

Despite the fact that treatise writers, theorists, and other people, through century after century, believed these "movements" to have been evils which had to be fought and eliminated, I am rather inclined to take a heretical point of view. More and more I have come to believe that the debasement of the petty coins and the failure to control their quantity did more good than harm.

Given the failure of Europe to adopt the state monopoly of issue and given its failure to discover an efficient device to control the quantity of petty coins in circulation, if it had tried to maintain these coins on a stable metallic content it would have suffered a disastrous and prolonged shortage of this type of currency. The debasement of the small coins was in those circumstances the only way to keep their supply reasonably elastic.

Moreover, during the Middle Ages the over-all supply of precious metals proved to be extremely inelastic in face of the continually growing demand for such metals for monetary and industrial purposes. Such states as might have maintained complete stability in the weight and alloy of the money which was also the base of their price system would have been struck by a deflation appalling for its duration century after century. On the other hand, for the Italian trading states, for instance, given their role and prestige in international trade and banking, it was extremely important to maintain the stability in weight and alloy of their pieces of gold money, their *fiorini* and *ducati*, which were the means of exchange in the international trade of the time. If those states managed to do this and to draw from the policy all its advantages while at the same time

[17] G. R. Carli, *Delle monete e dell'instituzione delle zecche d'Italia*, I (Mantua, 1754), pp. 337f.

escaping a great deflation, it was only because they had for purposes of internal circulation another series of coins which were continually being debased and a system of prices which rested upon these coins. In other words, the progressive debasement of the petty coins was, in the Mediterranean states, the economic safety valve which made possible the secular stability of the gold international currencies of the time.

An economic system within which circulate together an inflationary money and a stable money certainly holds particular interest for the economist as well as for the historian and the sociologist. The interest it can hold becomes still more intense if the society in which the phenomenon is found is sharply stratified and the two sorts of money tend to circulate in different social classes. This was the case in medieval Italy.

What I have called "petty coins" had in fact in the Mediterranean economy until the end of the Middle Ages a far greater role than for instance pennies, dimes, and quarters have in the present American economy. The price and wage levels in terms of silver were very much lower than today and retail trade was on a very small scale. Therefore, small coins were nearly the exclusive means of payment in local petty transactions. Wages were also usually fixed and paid in petty coins. This was possible, though, not only because the price and wage level was low in terms of silver, but also because there were generally no effective legal tender limitations on small coins; or, if there were such legal limitations, they were not really enforced.

While the workers were paid with small coins, the big merchants and entrepreneurs selling their products usually wanted to be paid with the gold coins.[18] In such a condition,

[18] Such a contrast was enforced also by law in industrial centers like Florence; see *Statuto del Podestà*, edited by R. Caggese (Florence, 1921), pp. 279-280, lib. III, rubr. 128, and A. Sapori, *Studi di storia economica medievale* (Florence, 1946), p. 671, n. 1. An interesting example of a merchant's refusing to accept payment in small coins can be found in G. Padovan, "L'attività commerciale di un patrizio Veneziano del Quattrocento," *Rivista di storia economica*, 8 (1943), p. 8.

given the usual lag of nominal wages behind the deterioration of the petty coins and the consequent rise of gold coins and commodity prices, any debasement of the petty coins provoking a depreciation of the petty coins in terms of the gold ones and in terms of commodities resulted, in the short run at least, in (1) a decrease of real wages and (2) an inflation of the profits of the entrepreneurs even if the selling prices of their products on the market did not increase in terms of the big gold coins.[19] It was natural, therefore, that the two classes of entrepreneurs and workers strongly opposed each other on the monetary question, the first backing a policy of debasement of the petty coins, the second a policy of stabilization. Evidence of such a contrast is continually recurring in the medieval records. Among the various instances that can be recalled, I think the most interesting is the one that refers to the events that happened in Florence after 1378.

The fourteenth century was one of social unrest for all Europe. Such unrest proved to be particularly acute in the most industrialized areas. In 1378 in Florence a popular revolution broke out; the businessmen's government was overthrown and a new government was created with a large participation of representatives of the wage-earning class. In the first days of the new government the popular representatives started the debate on the petty currency. In the beginning their efforts seem to have been in the direction of not allowing any further depreciation of the petty coins.[20] But later on they went further and began to advocate deflation. With these views in mind, they worked out a plan that they submitted to vote on October 24, 1380. In its essential lines the plan envisioned that, beginning on the first of January, 1381, and then consecutively for eight more years, the administration had to withdraw from circulation and melt down 2,000 *fiorini* worth of petty coins (*quat-*

[19] For a detailed analysis of the process see Cipolla, *Studi di storia della moneta*, pp. 121-123, and Cipolla, *Les mouvements monétaires*, pp. 24f.

[20] See the *provvigioni* of January 24, 1379, quoted in N. Rodolico, *La democrazia fiorentina nel suo tramonto* (Bologna, 1905), p. 266.

*trini*).[21] Such a proposal clearly indicated that those who prepared it fully realized that by restricting the quantity of the petty money in circulation they could increase its face value and keep its face value above the commodity value. The aim was to increase real wages, at least in the short run, without modifying nominal wages, and the maneuver was certainly well thought out to achieve that end. It does not seem that these people had even a vague idea of the unemployment which their measures could create. Yet their plan, while it throws light on the struggle between capital and labor in fourteenth century Florence, certainly remains one of the earliest conscious and logical attempts to control the value of money through the control of its quantity.

By vote in the Council of the *Popolo* (the organ of the party organization of the lesser merchants and laborers) the plan was approved 167 to 82. Two days later it was presented to the general Council of the Commune. Before it was voted on, an amendment was formulated by Benedetto degli Alberti, one of the aristocratic financiers in the government. The amendment added that the executives should enforce the plan only if the value of the petty coins should drop below where it was at the moment. The amendment was accepted. Practically it was a compromise between the deflation advocated by the popular party and the inflation backed by the big businessmen. The compromise was one of intrinsic stability. However, the next year the new government was overthrown, the popular party was defeated, and the big business elements regained full control. The first step was the abolition of both the plan and its amendment. And the debasement of the petty coins began again its secular course.[22]

With the beginning of modern times the social implications of the petty coins were completely changed. Through a progressive secular debasement the small coins were now

[21] Rodolico, *La democrazia fiorentina*, p. 256.

[22] For a complete account of the story see Rodolico, *La democrazia fiorentina*, pp. 256, 266, and Rodolico, "Il sistema monetario e le classi sociali nel Medioevo," *Rivista Italiana di Sociologia*, 8 (1904), pp. 462-469.

reduced to very low units of value. On the other side, through the sixteenth century, the general level of prices and wages moved markedly upward. Consequently, during the sixteenth century it became more and more common to see gold *scudi* or gold *ducati* or big silver *ducatoni* in the hands of the wage-earning people, just as it became more and more common to see these pieces used as means of payment in local and petty transactions.

The gold coins lost the character of "aristocratic money." Their "democratization" was indicative of the direction in which the times were moving. On the other side, the petty coins saw their role reduced more and more and limited to that area and those proportions to which we are today accustomed.[23]

[23] It could be misleading to call the petty coins "fractional money" before modern times. As we will see in the next chapter, the petty coins were often the real basic units of the prevailing systems of accounts.

# CHAPTER IV

## GHOST MONEYS

FOR centuries the people of Western Europe went on using monetary terms such as *libra* (pound), *solidus* (shilling), *denarius* (penny), and *florenus* (florin) in fixing the prices of their commodities and services, in establishing any sort of debts, or in keeping their accounts. Everybody used those terms and carried on transactions in them; everybody, from the wealthy merchant to the poor widow, from the learned *notarius* to the ignorant peasant, talked daily, made calculations, or kept calculations in pounds, shillings, pennies, florins, ducats, and so on. Yet, and here the mystery begins, during the greatest part of the Middle Ages and the first centuries of the modern period, with the exception of a few short periods, nobody ever saw many of those "moneys" about which everybody talked. For instance, nobody for centuries ever saw a real pound, for the simple, but paradoxical, reason that the pound during the greatest part of its life did not materialize into a real, visible, and touchable coin. It was a ghost money.

Strange as it may be, this is only the beginning of the mystery. People were very often accustomed to express prices and debts in terms of florins. The florin was actually a gold coin, of a given weight and alloy, a piece that everybody could see and touch as today everybody can see and touch a dime or half-dollar. But very often the florin about which the people were talking was not the real, material, nice piece of gold in circulation; very often it was another "money" that did not exist, which nobody could see or touch—a ghost money again. This strange story I am relating about the florin could also be told for the shillings, the groats, the ducats, and so on. It is important to make it clear that in all these cases the values attributed to the two "moneys," the real coin and the ghost, were *not* the

38

same. So that those who study the old papers and the old documents, when confronted with monetary expressions, must always keep in mind this question: "Does that monetary expression mean real money or ghost money?" Sometimes the documents are clear enough to allow a safe conclusion. When, for instance, they say *floreni auri et in auro* they generally mean a real, visible coin, a good piece of gold. But often they do not give a qualification at all, and expressions like *floreni* can mean either the real gold coin (with a certain value) or the ghost (with a different value).

The problem with which this chapter is concerned is that of the origins and the reasons for the existence of the ghost moneys. Because the subject is very broad and open to many and various interests, I cannot but try to give a very general and rather superficial outline of a very long, a very complicated, and in many points still obscure and mysterious story.

As a matter of fact, the question of the so-called "money of account"[1] (our ghost money) has been for centuries at the very core of the discussions and the debates on both monetary policy and theory. Innumerable books, articles, and pamphlets have been written on the subject, but I am strongly inclined to say that until the nineteenth century people did not have very clear ideas on it. If we want to know something about the matter, we must look first of all at the original documents, the monetary ordinances, the account books of the old merchants and trading companies, the notarial contracts, the registers of the old banks, the books of the mints, and the old monetary legislation. There, and only there, is the main clue to a solution of the mystery.

The final Carolingian reform based the monetary system of Mediterranean Europe on the silver penny. For three centuries from that time, the penny and the penny alone was the official denomination that the western mints coined for monetary purposes. The weight of the penny was finally

[1] About the expression "money of account" used in reference to the medieval pounds, shillings, ducats, and florins, see pp. 50f., n. 8.

determined in this way: out of a *libra* (pound) of pure silver 240 pennies had to be struck. The pound was then the usual unit of weight in use.

Since Roman times it was also usual to express debts and prices in terms of *solidi* (shillings), and the *solidi* were the prevailing money of account at the moment of the Carolingian reforms. In their final state these reforms asserted that twelve of the newly coined pennies were to be considered equivalent to one shilling. In its mature form, the system modeled by the Carolingian reforms was therefore based on these equivalents:

1 pound = 20 shillings = 240 pennies

Actually the pound was not a coin but a weight of silver. The shilling was an old name and unit introduced into the reform to link the new money with the immediate past and to facilitate its insertion into the system of already established debts. The penny finally was the only real money, the only real coin of the group.

Actually it was not a great coin. It was certainly not very artistically designed. And—this is the point that interests us—it represented a small unitary value. Using modern standards we can say that the penny in the ninth century weighed around 1.7 grams of silver. It is true that silver in those days had a much greater purchasing power than it has today. But it is clear that the penny represented a small unitary value. As a matter of fact, most of the transactions were on a very small scale, and the penny was quite suitable for them. But naturally some transactions were of another sort and required large amounts of money. For these, pennies proved to be rather cumbersome and inadequate. The prices had to be reckoned and paid in terms of tens of thousands or hundreds of thousands. The drawback was more serious in reckoning and accounting than it was in paying. In paying the drawback was felt less because in those days, as we have seen in the previous chapters, payments were not often made in specie; instead, other goods of equivalent value were used. Also the drawback was less important because people occasionally could pay in large foreign denominations like the Moslem *dinar* or *dirhem* or the Byzantine *nomisma*. Foreign coins or barter, in a word, proved useful substitutes to avoid payments of tens of thousands or hundreds of thousands of small coins. But the difficulty still remained for reckoning and accounting. It was to overcome this difficulty that people began more and more frequently to use the term "pound" to mean 240 pennies, the pound being actually the weight, as I said before, out of which 240 pennies were expected to be struck. In other words people instead of saying "240 pennies" found it easier to say "1 pound," transforming what was indicative of a total weight into a monetary expression. Just the same, the expression *solidus* was kept to mean 12 pennies.[2] In this way, instead of saying or writing, for instance, "14,412 pennies" people simply used "60 pounds and 1 shilling," which was much more easily done. The transformation would probably still seem elaborate to some of us, accustomed as we are to the metrical system. But the British, who still use the pound-shilling-penny system, assert that, once one is accustomed to it, the device is not particularly complicated; it certainly eliminates the big totals in pennies. So the ghost moneys began their life, and their appearance showed the basic need for a system of different denominations—a need that any society has, for denominations not only for actual payments, but also for accounting and reckoning purposes. By way of analogy, I would say that the shilling and the pound owed their birth and their life as units of account to the same kind of need that in our society induces us to use "miles" together with "inches" and "feet" for measurement. They were devices created and adopted to make the accounts easier. And since the governments did not provide society with a regular supply of differentiated denominations, people were forced to con-

[2] It must be noted, however, that the term *solidus*, when referring to a gold shilling, meant a real gold coin, which in the course of time could be worth more than 12 pennies.

tinue adopting abstract units to escape the inconvenience and the confusion of too large numbers.

In the progress of time the pennies, for reasons that would take too long to explain, were more and more debased. On the other hand, people went on using the expression *pound* as equivalent to "240 pennies." The consequence is clear. If at the beginning 240 pennies represented 1 real pound of silver, after the pennies began to drop in weight 240 of them represented less than 1 pound of silver. The pound-tale, therefore, ceased to be equal to the pound-weight. The ghost had begun its life, independent of the real being, from which it had borrowed its name.

With the tenth century the debasement of the pennies grew faster and faster, particularly in Mediterranean Europe. On the other side, the great long-term economic expansion of Western Europe made transactions for large amounts more and more frequent. Therefore the pennies proved more and more impractical. Their inability to perform the new needs of economic life was now more deeply felt since the barter practices of the previous period, particularly for payments and exchanges, became more and more infrequent and difficult to carry on in the framework of the growing division of labor.

With the end of the twelfth and even more during the thirteenth century one state after another began to issue denominations greater than the penny. Genoa around 1172 issued a silver coin worth 4 pennies of the standard then current. Florence and Rome soon followed the example of Genoa. Venice later in the twelfth century began to strike a piece rated at 24 pennies. In 1252 Florence again coined the gold florin equivalent to 240 local pennies, therefore materializing the local pound. In Genoa, at the same time, a gold piece was struck equivalent to about 120 local pennies, i.e. to half a pound. The example could be multiplied for all other Italian states. But the new developments were not limited to the Italian peninsula. In France, for instance, in 1266, during the reign of Louis IX, a gold coin was issued designed to represent one-half of the pound. A silver coin was also struck at a value of 1 shilling or 12 pennies.[3] A complete series of monetary units was thus created which represented the half-pound, the shilling, and the penny. At that moment all ghosts became real and everybody could actually touch and see and dispose of all denominations generally needed and used for accounting and paying.

That happy moment when the ghosts materialized and let themselves be touched and seen by everybody did not last for a long time. Very soon the ghosts left their material features and began again their mysterious, invisible life. Even more, they began to multiply and give birth to a numerous family of other ghosts. What was actually happening? And why?

To answer these questions, we have to recall what we said in the previous chapters. The monetary authorities of the Middle Ages and of the early modern age failed to discover completely the rules for maintaining stable relations of exchange between the pennies and the larger denominations. So for instance the gold coin that was struck in Genoa in 1252 and that at its appearance was rated at 120 Genoese pennies was equivalent to about 720 pennies at the beginning of the sixteenth century. The gold florin that was struck in Florence in 1252 with a value of 240 Florentine pennies was in 1500 evaluated at 1,680 pennies and by the beginning of the eighteenth century at about 3,192 pennies. Precisely why and how that inflationary movement developed is a matter that I cannot discuss in this chapter. What matters for the arguments that I am developing at present are the consequences of the instability for accounting practices.

Suppose we must register in our entry book the accounts for three days, not necessarily successive:

| day | florins | pennies |
|---|---|---|
| first | 3 | 180 |
| second | 9 | 140 |
| third | 1 | 160 |

[3] For all this see A. P. Usher, *The Early History of Deposit Banking in Mediterranean Europe* (Cambridge, Mass., 1943), pp. 206ff.

If on the three days the ratio between florins and pennies is always the same, let us say 240 pennies for 1 florin, the account is very easily kept: one adds the pennies, divides the total (in our case 480) by 240, and adds the result (in our case 2) to the column of florins. The final result in our case would be 15 florins and no pennies. In such a case people would not need to create abstract denominations larger than the penny to avoid the trouble of dealing continuously with too large numbers. The real florin could play this role of larger denominations.

But, as we have seen, the rule in that period, aside from limited exceptions, was that the rate of exchange between florins and pennies was continually fluctuating.

Let us take our example again and suppose that on the first day the rate of exchange was 240 pennies for 1 florin, the second day 250 pennies for 1 florin, and the third day 255 pennies for 1 florin. In such a case the addition grows rather difficult and one solution is to transform day by day, according to the daily rate, the florins into pennies and then make the addition in terms of pennies. In our case the operation would give the following results:

first day:
3 florins × 240 pennies =   720 + 180 =   900 pennies
second day:
9 florins × 250 pennies = 2,250 + 140 = 2,390 pennies
third day:
1 florin  × 255 pennies =   255 + 160 =   415 pennies
                              total   = 2,705 pennies

The operation is certainly not difficult, but it leaves the accountant to deal again with a total in pennies, with all the disadvantages to which we have referred before. If one wanted to use the real florins as larger denominations to express the total with simpler numbers, what kind of florin would one have to choose? The first-day florin at the rate of 240 or the second-day florin at the rate of 250 or the third-day florin at the rate of 255 pennies? In the case of hoarded money, if at the end of the third day one would know the present value of his monetary assets, he would have to add the florins, then add the pennies and divide the pennies total by the rate of exchange prevailing at the end of the third day. In this case the real florin could be used as a larger denomination of account to express the total. But this case was not the general one. The general case comprised money received and spent, and spent at different times during the three days. What could be done in such a case?[4]

Given the difficulty of using the real florins as larger denominations of account because of the instability of the rate of the florin, one solution was to keep alive the old ghosts, "pound" and "shilling," which by definition were always equal respectively to 240 pennies and 12 pennies. Using this device, the total of our example instead of being expressed as 2,705 pennies would be expressed as 11 pounds, 5 shillings, and 5 pennies.

Properly interpreted, this story teaches us another important lesson: for accounting purposes, it is necessary not only to possess a system of different denominations, but also to have a fixed and stable ratio among the different denominations. Since the monetary authorities of those times failed to maintain stable ratios between the different real denominations, people continued to use the ghost denominations, which by definition maintained a stable ratio between each other and between each of them and the basic real penny.

[4] For accounting purposes one must not overlook the importance of denominations of account larger than the penny. The example in the text is composed of only three items, the quantities of florins included are very small, and the rates of exchange between florins and pennies are among the lowest in the Middle Ages. Yet the total makes a figure in thousands. With more items, with larger and more realistic quantities of florins included in the account, with ratios of exchange that rated the florin at 1,000 pennies and even more at the end of the Middle Ages, the numbers with which one had to work would be extraordinary, if one expressed the total in pennies. The argument that I am developing is not based on hypothetical assumptions; it is sufficient to open any account book of the period and to express the totals in pennies; the number of that period would have been as impracticable as our prices and the totals of our accounts if we expressed them only in cents rather than in dollars and cents.

Thus far I have referred to those units that were called pound and shilling. There were also florins and ducats which were abstract multiple units, and which had nothing to do with the real coins known under the same names. I have briefly referred to these other ghosts at the beginning of the chapter. It is time now to look at them more closely. They, I believe, also confirm the points of view expressed in this chapter.

In different states, at different times, and because of more or less fortuitous circumstances among which one can include the movements of the market prices of gold and silver, the general economic situation, the monetary policy, and so on, it happened that the rate of exchange between the gold florin (or the gold ducat) and the local penny remained stable for a considerable length of time. This stability was rather exceptional in the general development of the monetary history of the Middle Ages. Yet in some periods it did exist, and for the matter which interests us it had significant consequences.

In Milan and its state, for instance, the florin was rated at 120 imperial pennies when it was first struck in 1252. The rate began very soon to rise and about 1340 the florin was rated at 384 pennies. At this moment the upward movement stopped and the rate remained stable until the end of the century.[5] For about sixty years Milan therefore had at its disposal a real, large monetary denomination in stable relation to the basic penny. According to what I have said earlier in the chapter, in such a condition the Milanese people would have used the real gold florin as the larger denomination of account. As a matter of fact this is what happened. The real florin became also the usual and popular unit of account in which debts of a certain size were expressed. Yet the pound and particularly the shilling did not disappear, because they also represented useful denominations between the penny and the florin. So the system of denominations of account in the state of Milan, which until

[5] C. M. Cipolla, *Studi di storia della moneta: I movimenti dei cambi in Italia dal sec. XIII al XV* (Pavia, 1948), p. 32.

the middle of the fourteenth century was composed of *three* denominations, pound, shilling, and penny, developed further in the second half of the same century and was composed of *four* denominations in the following stable relations:

florin = 1.6 pounds = 32 shillings = 384 pennies
pound = 20 shillings = 240 pennies
shilling = 12 pennies
penny

Of these four units, two were ghosts (the shilling and the pound), while two (the florin and the penny) were actually represented by real coins. Debts were usually expressed in florins, shillings, and pennies. Occasionally, when the relationship demanded it, pounds, shillings, and pennies were used.

With the beginning of the fifteenth century the long stability of the rates of exchange between florin and penny came to an end and the rate began again its upward movement.[6] In such a condition it was impossible to go on with the new system. We have noted earlier the difficulties in the use of denominations that are in no stable relation to each other. On the other hand, the florin had already become a common and popular money of account, used by everybody in the account books and in everyday business transactions. Use and tradition are a powerful force in monetary matters. It was difficult to get rid of the florin as a unit of account.

The solution to the problem developing from the contrasting tendencies, a solution not enforced by any law or decree but just spontaneously arising by the force of the events and the strength of the tradition, was that people continued to use the term "florin" to mean 384 pennies (i.e. 32 shillings) just as for centuries they had used the word "pound" to mean 240 pennies. Actually, after the beginning of the fifteenth century there was no real coin in the state of Milan worth 384 pennies. The florin worth 384 pennies was a ghost, an abstract multiple unit. The real

6 Cipolla, *Studi di storia della moneta*, p. 34.

florin was rated much higher, but at always fluctuating values. Around 1445, for instance, it was rated at about 768 pennies; at that time therefore 1 real florin was worth 2 ghost florins. And the difference became greater in the course of time.

The example I quoted from the monetary history of the state of Milan was not an isolated case. On the contrary, I quoted it because it was a common case and it offers a good illustration of what was happening in many places. In Genoa, for instance, in the fourteenth century the gold florin remained stable for about seventy years at the rate of 300 pennies (25 shillings). When the rate began to increase again in the second decade of the fifteenth century, the people retained the florin of 300 pennies as an abstract unit of account. In Venice the gold ducat in the second half of the fifteenth century remained stable on the quota of 124 shillings for more than forty years. When in 1517 the rate of the gold ducat again began to move upward, people retained the use of the ducat of 124 shillings as an abstract unit of account.

Other examples could be given, but they would add nothing to what has been said. Rather than quote them, I would like to point out a circumstance that is apparent from the examples already quoted. The terms "pound" and "shilling" had a universally identical meaning: everywhere, in Genoa as in Milan, in Florence as in Barcelona or Marseilles, they respectively meant "240" and "12." The pennies to which they referred were not the same; but the number of pennies they meant was everywhere and always the same. This was not true for the florins of account. The term "florin" used as an abstract multiple unit did not have the same meaning everywhere, its value in terms of real pennies being determined by the actual value of the real florin when the real florin had a long period of stability in its relation with the penny. So in Milan the florin of account meant 32 shillings (or, which is the same, 384 pennies), in Genoa it meant 25 shillings (or 300 pennies), and so on.

Actually, the periods of long stability in the ratio of exchange between florins or ducats or other big coins and the local pennies gave also the opportunity for the solution of a problem different from the one to which I have referred. Let us take for a general illustration of the other solution the case of Florence. Here for a certain period in the second half of the thirteenth century the florin remained stable at the rate of 348 (real) pennies i.e. 29 (ghostly) shillings. When the rate began to move again, instead of retaining the pennies as the basis of the system of account and using the shilling, the pound, and the florin of 384 pennies as a large ghostly multiple unit of account, the Florentine merchants just reversed the solution. They kept the real florin as the basis of their system of account, and for expressing fractions of the florin they retained the denominations of shilling and pennies to mean respectively $\frac{1}{29}$ and $\frac{1}{384}$ of a florin. Actually these pennies and these shillings were now ghostly units. The ghost penny equal to $\frac{1}{384}$ of the real florin was not only different from, but also more valuable than, the real penny, which was always a smaller and smaller fraction of the real florin. And therefore the ghost shilling which represented 12 times the ghost penny (or $\frac{1}{29}$ of the real florin) was a unit different from and more valuable than the ghost shilling which represented 12 times the real penny. At this point the reader may have the impression that the ghosts were bringing confusion all around.

The type of solution that kept the real florin as the base of the system of account was most suited to the big merchants, whose business was carried on in terms of gold florins. The small retail traders and the common people retained the other type of accounting system, the one based on the real penny.

It seems clear from what has been stated that every coin could be taken as a basis of an accounting system. Once people had chosen no matter what coin as base money, and since no real fixed multiple or fractions existed in stable relation to the chosen base money, people created around it a structure of abstract denominations to express its multiples or its fractions. If the coin chosen as a base money was a small one, people needed and created a system of abstract multiples. If the coin chosen as a base money was a big one, people needed and created a system of abstract fractions. As has been clearly stated, there prevailed then a typical "habit of mind that made possible the building of a system of account upon any coin whenever the conveniences of reckoning might so be suited."[7] In developing these abstract systems of different denominations people always used the terms "pound" and "shilling" to mean respectively "240 times" and "12 times." When they had to develop a system of multiples, the terms "pound" and "shilling" meant respectively "240 times" and "12 times" the real base money, usually the real penny. When they had to develop a system of fractions, the penny was a given ghostly fraction of a real big coin (florin or ducat) and "pound" and "shilling" meant respectively "240 times" and "12 times" the given ghostly fraction.

It follows from what has been said that all the systems of account in existence in those days were actually based on and tied to a real coin. From an economic point of view it is important to emphasize that there existed side by side systems of account based on stable base moneys (like the ducat or the florin) and systems of account linked to progressively deteriorating base moneys (like the different types of pennies). The prevalence in any given society by custom or by law of one system or of the other as the usual and common system of account had decisive effects in the relations between debtors and creditors and on the social dynamics; the prevalence of a system based on a stable coin was favorable to creditors and *rentiers*, the prevalence of a system based on a deteriorating coin was favorable to debtors and entrepreneurs.

These in broad outline were the reasons for and the characteristics of the so-called "moneys of account"[8] in the

---

[7] A. Evans, "Some Coinage Systems of the Fourteenth Century," *Journal of Economic and Business History*, 3 (1931), p. 490.

[8] The term "money of account" is not very exact and rather misleading. Usher, *The Early History of Deposit Banking*, p. 201, has already pointed out that "some writers have described this reckoning as 'money

greatest part of the Middle Ages. Their birth and their life were due to the failure of the monetary authorities to keep in circulation pieces of different denomination in rational and stable relation to each other, and to the need for such a system of different denominations in any rational accounting.

---

of account' and spoken of it as imaginary money. The terms are misleading and inaccurate. Accounts were kept in terms of these units; they were units of value, but they were never means of payment. Credit kept in such units may serve as means of payment, but the units were merely accounting units. They may be correctly described as denominations of account." However, Usher's term "denomination of account" can be similarly misleading because it can imply an independent unit of value. (See also M. Bloch, *Esquisse d'une histoire monétaire de l'Europe* [Paris, 1954], p. 25.)

# CHAPTER V

# PRICES AND CIVILIZATION

SOME years ago Sir William Beveridge, in an introduction to his inquiry into the history of prices and wages in England from the twelfth to the nineteenth century, wrote that "in the study of modern prices, determination of the general level of prices and its movements has bulked largely. Prices have been considered mainly as means of throwing light on monetary problems; the construction of index numbers for all commodities or for a few main groups of commodities, has been an early task. In the present work the emphasis is different. Price-relatives for single commodities, rather than index-numbers for commodities in combination, are the main objective. Index numbers do not appear [here]; their construction over periods as vast as those covered by this history presents problems of weighting for which there is no easy, indeed no general, solution. At Hinderclay in Suffolk, before the Black Death, wheat was being sold at prices varying with the harvest but ranging about 5 shillings a quarter; steel was being bought for ploughshares and other implements at prices also varying from year to year and ranging about £. 50 and upward per ton. Today a normal price for wheat is about 50 shillings a quarter and for steel is about £. 10 a ton. While the price of wheat has multiplied ten times, that of steel has fallen to a fifth; a quarter of wheat will buy fifty times as much steel as once it did. The contrast between the wheat age and the steel age could hardly be better illustrated." And further on he concluded: "Whether the period chosen be short or long, price history is a study not of isolated facts but of relations; comparison is its essence."[1]

I wish to use the same type of analysis for some prices and price relationships in Mediterranean Europe with par-

[1] W. Beveridge, *Prices and Wages in England from the Twelfth to the Nineteenth Century* (London, 1939), pp. xxvf.

ticular reference to the period between the end of the thirteenth century and the beginning of the modern age. Unfortunately we cannot hope for statistical precision. Data are scanty for the period, and furthermore their nature and type do not permit the application of modern statistical devices and standards. We therefore must be satisfied with approximations and generalizations. Neither the method nor the results are completely satisfactory, but the data permit no more.

A long and world-wide historical experience has emphasized the strategic importance of transportation in the growth, development, and modeling of civilizations. I begin, therefore, with a discussion of transportation.

In the early Middle Ages few but significant facts are witnesses to the enormous cost of transportation. In southern Italy before the eleventh century the use of a wagon cost as much as 3 or 5 acres of good land.[2] In France the monks of the abbey of Corbie, facing the problem of transporting hay from their farms to the monastery, were forced to remark very sorrowfully indeed that "not only is it hard, it is even impossible, to get carried to the monastery from outlying holdings the grains or the hay which has been harvested without the very greatest overburdening of the monastery's dependents."[3]

After the tenth century, progress was undoubtedly made. Roads and bridges were more numerous and they were improved and better maintained, so that travel was safer. Courts, procedures, and customs were created and perfected, all designed to protect and regulate local and international transportation. Technical improvements were made in both the organization and the means of transport, by land and by sea. The establishment of inns for travelers and of stables for their animals also facilitated travel, especially after the beginning of the twelfth century. But in spite of all improvements transportation remained difficult

[2] A. Lizier, *L'economia rurale dell'età prenormanna nell'Italia meridionale* (Palermo, 1907), p. 16.
[3] *Statuta antiqua Abbatiae Corboliensis* in *Le polyptyque de l'Abbé Irminon*, edited by B. E. Guerard (Paris, 1844), II, p. 324.

and costly. Land transport was in a particularly disadvantageous position. Given the shape and the geographical physiognomy of a good part of Europe, forested or mountainous or intersected by a great many streams, the use of wheeled vehicles was often impossible until a satisfactory network of roads had been established. Main routes that allowed the use of wheeled vehicles were few.

Wagons were used for short local hauls, generally by farmers, and for longer hauls by military forces; as early as the thirteenth century they were also used to carry merchandise from southern to northern France. But, allowing for these exceptions, we can still say that the normal means of transport *over long distances* was, until the late Middle Ages the pack mule.[4]

Transportation by pack mule, however, was expensive since the unit load on a mule weighed between 300 and 400 pounds. Such transportation was also very slow; in general, freight moved at an average speed of around 15 to 25 miles a day.[5] These technical elements made the costs very high, but to them were added other factors, of different sorts, which rendered transportation costs still higher. Given the extreme political and administrative fragmentation of Europe in those centuries, a merchant with his pack mule and wares had to stop every little while to pay the *gabelle* or *telonei* or *dazii* (or some other form of toll and custom) to a city or to a landlord. Added together these numerous *gabelle* and *telonei* came to represent a sizable sum.

No wonder, therefore, that men of the time tried whenever possible to avoid land transportation and to follow instead the water routes, by sea when that was possible or

---

[4] R. H. Bautier, "Les registres des foires de Champagne," *Bulletin philologique et historique* (1945), p. 172. Transportation of cloth by wagon was forbidden. Cloths could be transported only "cum bestiis sine carrataxio." See also P. Wolff, *Commerce et marchands de Toulouse* (Paris, 1954), pp. 449-450.

[5] On the average speed of travel and transportation in the Middle Ages see F. Ludwig, *Untersuchungen über die Reise-und Marschgeschwindigkeit im XII. und XIII. Jahrhundert* (Berlin, 1897); C. M. Cipolla, "In tema di trasporti medievali," *Bollettino storico Pavese*, 7 (1944), p. 32; R. H. Bautier, "Les registres des foires de Champagne," p. 174; P. Wolff, *Commerce et marchands de Toulouse*, pp. 450-451.

by river. It is amazing to note how those men used freight boats on rivers or little tributaries which no one today would ever dream of navigating. As a matter of fact a river boat could always carry more than a pack mule, and that would mean a reduction in costs. Moreover, when transportation was downstream with the current, it was faster than land transport and that meant there was an additional reduction in costs.

Transport by sea had still other advantages. Above all, there was the carrying capacity of the ship. A Mediterranean galley in the fifteenth century could carry 150 to 250 tons. A great sailing ship could carry even more. At the beginning of the fifteenth century the Venetian round ships generally used for the Syrian voyage had a capacity of around 300 to 400 tons. Naturally, there were big exceptions—the "Queens" of those days. The *Paradisus Magnus*, one of the largest and most famous of the Genoese merchant vessels of the mid-thirteenth century, could carry as many as 600 tons, dead cargo weight. The *Roccaforte*, a big and famous Venetian vessel of the thirteenth century, could carry about 500 tons. Another Venetian ship, built at the beginning of the fifteenth century, could carry about 700 tons.[6]

Furthermore, on the sea one did not meet with those endless *gabelle* and *telonei* which one met on land and on the rivers. We do not have abundant or precise data from which to figure out the relative costs, but in an approximate way it has been calculated that at the end of the thirteenth century, other things being equal, sea transport cost only about a twentieth of land transport.[7]

Though maritime transportation cost much less than

[6] A. De Capmany y de Montpalau, *Memorias historicas sobre la marina, comercio y artes de la antiqua ciudad de Barcelona*, I (Madrid, 1779), p. 40; E. H. Byrne, *Genoese Shipping in the Twelfth and Thirteenth Centuries* (Cambridge, Mass., 1930), pp. 10-11; F. C. Lane, *Venetian Ships and Shipbuilders of the Renaissance* (Baltimore, 1934), pp. 15, 39f.

[7] M. de Böuard, "Problèmes de subsistance dans un état médiéval: le marché et les prix des céréales au royaume angevin de Sicile, 1266-1282," *Annales d'histoire économique et sociale*, 10 (1938), p. 489.

land transportation it was still a rather expensive business. The ships needed large crews for defense and operation. In the case of the Venetian galleys, for instance, Professor Lane of Johns Hopkins has pointed out that the large size of the crews was the chief reason for the high freight rates which were charged.[8]

In the second half of the Middle Ages, land and sea transportation was considerably improved and the cost was greatly reduced, but the expenses involved were still burdensome.[9] And when we add to the already-mentioned factors the element of risk, increased by the bandits on the highways and the pirates on the sea, and by the frequent state of war, we can easily understand the reasons for the high freight rates.

The transportation of wine from Pisa to Florence by river, a distance of about 50 miles, cost more than 50 per cent of the original price of the wine; and the wine was very good and not cheap. The transportation of salt on the same route cost more than 60 per cent of the original price of the salt. The carriage of grains from Armenia to southern Italy by sea cost more than 160 per cent. These percentages do not need much comment. Under those conditions and unless particular needs or situations arose, transportation was economically convenient only for precious and expensive merchandise. Transporting a precious slave from Pavia to Genoa, a distance of about 80 miles, cost at the end of the fourteenth century more than 15 grams of gold (and note that the purchasing power of the gold was much higher in those days than today); but given the very high price of the slave, the transportation cost did not represent more than 8 per cent of the original price. For the same reasons, it did not cost more than 2 per cent of the original price to send 4 bales of precious silk from Lucca (Tuscany) to Lagny (northern France) in 1302. In 1391 the transportation of rugs and silk from the Near East to South Italy by sea cost about 15 per cent. In 1321 and 1322, transporta-

[8] Lane, *Venetian Ships*, p. 28.
[9] Lane, *Venetian Ships*, p. 39 and passim.

tion by land of cloth from Flanders to Florence cost about 18 per cent. At the end of the fifteenth century sending spices from Genoa to Frankfurt could cost between 3 and 13 per cent of the original price according to the different types of spices.[10]

It seems to me that all these figures can explain some of the basic characteristics of that civilization. A curious mixture of universalism and particularism dominated the scene. It was economically convenient to get precious silk from China or precious rugs from the Near East, but it was usually not convenient to get poorer commodities from a few miles away. Since mass transportation was impossible for technical reasons, freight costs remained relatively high. Particularly when transportation by water route was impossible, long-distance trade had to rely mainly, if not exclusively, on precious objects. For its basic daily needs any community had always to be as self-sufficient and self-sustaining as possible. The interlocal division of labor had to rest mainly on precious objects or on things that by no means could be made locally or were not susceptible of easy substitution. And trade had to rest heavily on aristocratic consumption of luxury goods.

Communication and transfer of merchandise were difficult and expensive. No less difficult and expensive were the transfer and communication of ideas. Have you ever estimated the price of a book before the discovery of printing?

According to a Spanish document of 796 an antiphonary cost 3 gold *solidi*, a prayer book 2 gold *solidi*, and another book again 2 gold *solidi*. According to the same document an ox or a cow was worth 1⅓ *solidi*.[11] A book would cost

10 The figures quoted are taken from Cipolla, "In tema di trasporti medievali." P. Wolff, *Commerce et marchands de Toulouse*, p. 456, remarks that transportation of agricultural products was economically convenient only in times of famine when the prices of the products were particularly high. On the cost of transporting wine in the Middle Ages, see the very interesting observations of Y. Renouard, "La consommation des grands vins du Bourbonnais et de Bourgogne à la cour Pontificale d'Avignon," *Annales de Bourgogne*, 24 (1952), pp. 221-244.

11 C. Sánchez-Albornoz, "El precio de la vida en el Reino Astur-Leonés hace mil años," *Logos*, 3 (1945), pp. 225-264.

roughly as much as two cows: this would be considered an unusual ratio today.

For later periods the documents are more abundant and more nearly accurate. To make the comparisons more precise I will take the documents from a well-determined geographical area. The place that I choose is Pavia, a Lombard town, famous in the Middle Ages for its great university.

For the fourteenth century we have inventories of three private libraries in Pavia. The first is the inventory of the library of a medical doctor, Sylanus Niger, who was also a professor in the university. His library was composed of thirty volumes of *materia medica* and was estimated to be worth 133½ gold florins. The most expensive volumes were appraised at 12 florins each. The cheapest ones were valued at 1 florin each. The greatest frequency of values is in the class of 1 to 5 florins. The general average is 4.5 florins per volume.[12] The second library is that of a lawyer, Jacobus de Ascheriis, also a professor in the local university. We do not know the exact number of books that he possessed, because the inventory is not complete, but we know of fifteen books of that library. These fifteen books, all of a legal nature, were appraised at a total of 385 florins. The greatest frequency of values was between 10 and 25 florins. The general average was 25.7 florins per volume. The third library is that of Signor Pinotto de Pinotti, a wealthy lawyer, who also had important political connections and functions. His library was composed of forty-six volumes, but we are told the values of only thirty-two of them. These volumes were worth 569 florins, with an average of 17.8 florins per volume. The nature of the content seems to have been very heterogeneous indeed. But if we take only those volumes which deal with law, we arrive at an average of 29.3 florins per volume, a figure which is near to the average we found for the law books of Jacobus de Ascheriis. The other books of the Pinotti library, of a

---

[12] The term "book" when dealing with medieval manuscripts is ambiguous; all instances dealt with in this chapter concern bound volumes.

moralistic and religious nature, show an average worth of about 14 florins per volume.[13]

For the middle of the fifteenth century other documents give us further evidence.[14] In 1449 the abbot of the Monastery of Santa Cristina in Pavia went to Rome and there bought four volumes of canon law, paying for them 250 florins, at an average of 62.5 florins per volume. In 1446 six volumes of law books were elsewhere appraised at 99 florins, with an average of 16.5 florins per volume. In 1449 ten volumes of legal books comprising the library of one of the wealthiest citizens of Pavia, Giovanni Marco Fiamberti, were valued at 380 florins, at an average of 38 florins per volume. Between 1455 and 1461 the main hospital of Pavia sold 44 law books which had been left to it in the wills of private benefactors. The sale brought to the hospital an average of 7 florins per volume.

These figures are not as contradictory as they seem at first glance. The books bought by the abbot in Rome in 1449 were precious volumes. The prices of the books sold by the hospital were prices obtained at a sort of public auction of secondhand goods. A more nearly normal valuation is reflected in the two averages of 38 and 16.5 florins mentioned earlier. The average of 38 florins was the appraised value of the books of one of the wealthiest aristocrats of the town; his books were probably very good copies, finely bound and well cared for. The average of 16.5 florins, in contrast, was for volumes of law books seized for the unpaid debts of a student. We are probably safe if we accept as a normal average the average between the two, i.e. a value of about 25 florins per volume for law books.

In 1461 the books on various subjects belonging to a wealthy Pavian merchant and man of affairs were appraised

[13] The three inventories were edited by C. M. Cipolla, "Il valore di alcune biblioteche nel Trecento," *Bollettino storico Pavese*, 7 (1944), pp. 5-20.

[14] See F. Borlandi, "Biblioteche Pavesi del Quattrocento," *Bollettino della Società Pavese di Storia Patria*, 46 (1947), pp. 43-87, and G. Aleati, "Biblioteche e prezzi di codici in Pavia nel tardo Medioevo," *Bollettino della Società Pavese di Storia Patria*, 49-50 (1951), pp. 99-107.

at an average of 16 florins per book. In 1485 two antiphonaries cost a total of about 32 florins.

Let us try to summarize. The evidence we have seems
to indicate that medical books were the least expensive,
with an average of about 4.5 florins per volume. Books on
varied subjects differed greatly in price, but in general
averaged between 15 and 30 florins per volume. The most
expensive were the books of law, costing around 25 to 30
florins per volume. These are averages. Then naturally,
single books on special subjects or with numerous illustrations and decorations could go up to 40, 60, 100 florins.

What do these figures mean? For a first estimate let us
try to express them in grams of gold. The florin was a piece
of pure gold with a weight of about 3.5 grams and it remained stable during the period under discussion. Therefore the average price for volumes of *materia medica* would
be about 15 grams of pure gold and for law books about
90 to 100 grams. Volumes of books on other subjects could
range between 50 and 100 grams per volume. However,
gold in those days had a much higher purchasing power
than it has today. So the figures in gold grams fail to give
a precise and correct idea of the cost of a book in that society and tend to undervalue it.

To overcome this difficulty let us bring into the picture
another element of comparison. In 1376 in Pavia a certain
Zanino attested by notarial act that he owed a man called
Borello 80 florins because the latter had supported Zanino,
for four years and two months, with all necessary provisions and clothing.[15] From this we can reckon that the
cost of living in Pavia toward the end of the fourteenth
century was about 20 florins per year per person. Zanino
and Borello were average people, so we can further deduce
that in this case we deal with an average standard of living.
From another notarial document of about a century later
we know that the complete maintenance of a boy (room and
board, clothing, and grammar school fees) cost 14 florins

[15] Cipolla, "Il valore di alcune biblioteche," p. 12.

a year.[16] Since many other data which we have seem to indicate that between the end of the fourteenth century and the end of the fifteenth century the general level of prices in terms of gold was going down, we may conclude that the two witnesses cited agree approximately, and this permits us to assume that in Pavia complete maintenance of an ordinary person cost around 20 florins a year late in the fourteenth century and a somewhat smaller sum in gold a century later.

If we accept this approximation, we must conclude that in the late fourteenth century the average price of a medical volume was equal to the living costs of an average person for around three months, and a law book cost as much as such a person's maintenance for one year and four months. In the course of the fifteenth century the ratio between these two items changed somewhat, making the cost of the books still higher.

These figures and the ratios I quoted represent averages; special volumes accentuated the discrepancies. The highest book price in our lists is that of 100 florins. The *Decretum Gratiani* belonging to Signor Pinotto de Pinotti was evaluated at that figure. The same quotation was given for the *Novelae super Sesto* belonging to Signor Iacobo de Ascheriis. At the end of the fourteenth century each of those books represented 350 grams of pure gold or the sum needed to maintain a person for five years.

Confronted with such figures we can understand why in 1392 the Countess of Blois, wife of the Baron of Castellane, willed to her daughter a parchment manuscript of the *Corpus Juris*, but made the specification that the daughter should marry a jurist in order that this valuable treasure could come into the right hands.

Let us now offer another standard of comparison, the salaries of the professors of the University of Pavia at that time. In 1435 the stipends of professors were determined in each particular case and ranged from *nichil* (nothing)

[16] Borlandi, "Biblioteche Pavesi," p. 54, n. 1.

to 200 florins. The general arithmetical average of all the stipends actually paid is 52 florins. But the average is influenced too much by the few cases of maximum salaries. If one looks at the frequency of cases in the various classes of salaries, one can see that out of 52 professors 36 got between "nothing" and 50 florins *per annum*. In 1447 the salaries varied between 7.5 and 300 florins. The average of all the salaries actually paid was 74.5 florins. Out of 76 professors 46 got salaries between 10 and 50 florins.[17] The range of variations and distributions is such that an over-all average has little meaning. But we can say that 64 per cent of the university professors in 1435 and 60 per cent in 1447 had salaries of less than 51 florins *per annum*. It is, therefore, safe to say that with his complete annual salary a professor in the lower-paid majority group could buy less than two books of law and less than ten books of medicine.

The accumulated evidence permits no other conclusion but that books were rather expensive. And they were expensive because they had to be written by hand. The making of two antiphonaries in Pavia in 1485 cost 19 florins for the miniatures and the binding, and all of 36 florins for the writing of words and music.[18] The excessive cost of production with the subsequent high price limited the size of private libraries. With the exception of monastic and princely libraries, private libraries varied usually between ten and fifty books. Though so small, they represented great fortunes. The library of the medical doctor Sylanus Niger, with its thirty volumes, was worth about 500 grams

[17] *Codice diplomatico della Università di Pavia* II (Pavia, 1913-1915), *sub anno*. In the original documents figures were expressed in florins of account. For purpose of comparison I transformed the florins of account into real gold florins, the prices of the book always having been calculated in terms of real florins.

[18] Borlandi, "Biblioteche Pavesi," p. 57. One can compare the figures quoted in the text with the following: in 1345 Etienne de Conty paid for a handsomely adorned copy of the *Commentaries* of Henry Bohic 62 *livres* and 11 *sous*; for the production of this work 35 *l.* and 5 *s.* was paid to the scribe, and 25 *l.* and 6 *s.* was paid for the parchment, the illuminations, and the binding. See G. H. Putnam, *Books and Their Makers during the Middle Ages* (London, 1896), p. 298.

of gold or the sum that covered a man's living expenses through seven years. Thirty-two of the forty-six volumes which comprised the private library of Signor Pinotto de Pinotti cost about 2 kilograms of gold and equaled the sum necessary for a person to live for twenty-eight years. The eighteen volumes valued at 300 florins, i.e. about 1 kilogram of gold, that the wealthy merchant Pietro de Buschis had in his house in 1461 represented more than one-fourth of the total value of his house furniture, jewelry, and working capital.[19]

Culture was expensive and its expensiveness helps to explain why for centuries it was mainly a sport of the aristocracies.

Another strategic price that deserves special attention is the price of money, actually the rate of interest. Throughout the Middle Ages in no part of Western Europe did people know the benefits of what we today call cheap money. Some evidence seems to point out that there existed an ultrasecular downward trend in the different types of rates of interest, at least after the end of the thirteenth century. At the end of the Middle Ages it seems that the price of money was generally on lower levels than it was, let us say, in the thirteenth and fourteenth centuries.[20] Yet, even toward the end of the Middle Ages, it was generally expensive to raise money.

For long-term loans to commercial towns or municipal governments like those of Barcelona, Genoa, or Florence, rates of interest were not exceedingly high. The rates of interest on the long-term loans to the commune of Florence in the fourteenth century ranged between 5 and 15 per cent.[21] The rates on the long-term loans to the city of Genoa in the fifteenth century ranged between 4 and 10

[19] Aleati, "Biblioteche e prezzi di codici," p. 107.
[20] A. P. Usher, *The Early History of Deposit Banking in Mediterranean Europe* (Cambridge, Mass., 1943), pp. 170-174.
[21] L. Cibrario, *Della economia politica del Medioevo* (Turin, 1861), III, p. 318, and A. Sapori, *Studi di storia economica medievale* (Florence, 1946), p. 49.

per cent.[22] The open-market rates on annuities issued by the city of Barcelona during the fifteenth century ranged between 4 and 5.5 per cent.[23]

Loans to kings or princes were rightly considered much riskier and the rates of interest in these cases were generally kept on a much higher level. The Emperor Frederick II usually had to pay 30 to 40 per cent interest to his creditors. In 1319 the Angevin King of Naples had to agree to 30 per cent with his Florentine lenders.[24] Sometimes the rates were even higher. Sometimes they were lower, as in the case of the long-term loans contracted by Ferdinand and Isabella in 1484 and 1489 at a rate of 10 per cent.[25]

The rates naturally varied according to the bargaining power of the two contracting parties and according to the risk involved in the operation, i.e. according to the amount of security which the borrower was able to put up. In 1328, for instance, the Duke of Calabria could obtain a loan of 6,000 florins from some Florentine merchants at 15 per cent, giving them precious jewels as security.[26]

For private business ventures, during the fourteenth and fifteenth centuries, merchants and entrepreneurs could get money at rates between 7 and 15 per cent. This at least was the normal range of rates through the fourteenth and fifteenth centuries in the Italian trading and industrial towns like Florence and Pisa.[27]

Loans for consumption purposes to average people naturally tended to cost much more, the higher cost mainly reflecting the higher risk involved for the lender. It is certainly possible to find cases in which the rate of interest exceeded 50 per cent, but they were not very frequent.

---

[22] H. Sieveking, "Studio sulle finanze genovesi nel Medioevo e in particolare nella Casa di San Giorgio," *Atti della Società Ligure di Storia Patria*, 35, parts 1 and 2 (1905-1906).

[23] Usher, *The Early History of Deposit Banking*, p. 171.

[24] R. Caggese, *Roberto d'Angiò e i suoi tempi*, I (Florence, 1922), p. 595.

[25] Usher, *The Early History of Deposit Banking*, p. 174.

[26] Caggese, *Roberto d'Angiò*, I, p. 595.

[27] For Florence see Sapori, *Studi di storia economica*, p. 49. For Pisa I have the information thanks to the kindness of Professor F. Melis.

Loans to consumers generally were made at from 15 to 50 per cent per year. This applies to the towns. In the country the rates charged were usually somewhat higher. Rents on land were usually capitalized in fifteenth century Lombardy at a 6 per cent rate, although it is not unusual to find lower or higher rates. In southern France, in the area of Toulouse, during the fifteenth century the prevailing rate was 10 per cent.[28]

Very broadly, this was the structure of interest rates in the last two centuries of the Middle Ages—a structure characterized, in comparison with that prevailing in modern Western societies, by an extraordinarily wider range of rates. Against these rates everybody voiced complaints, the moralists and theologians, the politicians and entrepreneurs, the men on the street and in the taverns. At least in the more developed areas, and quite apart from the treatises of the moralists and the theologians, complaints were directed not against the idea of interest in itself, but rather against the height of the current rates. Businessmen certainly emphasized the latter.[29] And the public powers tried desperately to fix a legal limit, with any higher rate declared to be usury. It is interesting to observe what the legal maximum was. In Milan at the end of the twelfth century it was established at 15 per cent.[30] The Emperor Frederick II tried to enforce a legal maximum of 10 per cent in Sicily. In Verona in 1228 the legal maximum was established at 12.5 per cent. In Modena in 1270 it was fixed at 20 per cent, and in Genoa at 15 per cent throughout the same century.[31] In France in 1311 it was fixed at 20 per cent.[32] In Lombardy in 1390 it was fixed at 10 per

[28] Wolff, *Commerce et marchands de Toulouse*, p. 358.

[29] See the interesting text edited by G. Corti, "Consigli sulla mercatura di un anonimo Trecentista," *Archivio storico Italiano*, 110 (1952), pp. 117-119.

[30] P. Verri, *Storia di Milano*, I (Milan, 1834), p. 314.

[31] Cibrario, *Della economia politica*, III, pp. 317f., and L. T. Belgrano, "L'interesse del denaro e le cambiali appo i Genovesi dal sec. XII al XV," *Archivio storico Italiano*, ser. 3, 3 (1866), p. 114.

[32] *Ordonnances des Roys de France de la troisième race*, edited by M. De Laurière, I (Paris, 1723), p. 485.

cent. In Western Europe at the beginning of the nineteenth century the legal maximum for the rate of interest was still enforced; but it was down to 5 per cent.

If one devotes oneself to the study of medieval civilization, one is struck by two characteristics: the fundamental particularism and the aristocratic character. To explain the first one cannot overlook what has been said in this chapter about the cost of transportation. To understand the second one must always keep in mind that the cost of books was prohibitive and that for the great mass of the people the price of money loans was exceedingly high.

These ideas are not very new. But I hope that I have presented several general standards by which we can measure and understand economic factors whose influence on the history of civilization should not be overlooked.

ONLY those books and articles appear to which reference has been made in this work.

## BOOKS AND ARTICLES RELATING TO THE HISTORY AND THEORY OF MONEY[1]

Bergmann, E. von, "Die Nominale der Münzreform des Chalifen Abdulmelik," *Sitzungsberichte der philosophisch-historischen Classe der Kaiserlichen Akademie der Wissenschaften*, 56 (1870), pp. 239-266.

Bloch, M., "Le problème de l'or au moyen âge," *Annales d'histoire économique et sociale*, 5 (1933), pp. 1-34.

Bloch, M., "Économie nature ou économie argent," *Annales d'histoire sociale*, 1 (1939), pp. 7-16.

Bloch, M., *Esquisse d'une histoire monétaire de l'Europe* (Paris, 1954).

Bognetti, G. P., "Il problema monetario dell'economia Longobarda e il panis e la scutella de cambio," *Archivio storico Lombardo*, new series, 9 (1944), pp. 112-120.

Cannan, E., *Money* (Westminster, 1929).

Carli, G. R., *Delle monete e dell'istituzione delle zecche d'Italia* (Mantua, 1754).

Carothers, N., *Fractional Money* (New York, 1930).

Cipolla, C. M., *Studi di storia della moneta: I movimenti dei cambi in Italia dal sec. XIII al XV* (Pavia, 1948).

Cipolla, C. M., *Les mouvements monétaires dans l'État de Milan, 1580-1700* (Paris, 1952).

Dieudonné, A., "Des especes de circulation internationale en Europe depuis Saint Louis," *Revue suisse de numismatique*, 22 (1920), pp. 3-39.

Dopsch, A., *Naturalwirtschaft und Geldwirtschaft in der Weltgeschichte* (Vienna, 1930).

Evans, A., "Some Coinage Systems of the Fourteenth Century," *Journal of Economic and Business History*, 3 (1931), pp. 481-496.

Grierson, P., "Problemi monetari dell'Alto Medioevo," *Bollettino della Società Pavese di Storia Patria*, 54 (1954), pp. 67-82.

[1] A most useful bibliography on the history of money has been published by P. Grierson, *Coins and Medals: A Select Bibliography* (London, 1954).

# BIBLIOGRAPHY

Grierson, P., "The Debasement of the Bezant in the Eleventh Century," *Byzantinische Zeitschrift*, 47 (1954), pp. 379-394.

Grierson, P., "Carolingian Europe and the Arabs: The Myth of the *Mancus*," *Revue Belge de Philologie et d'Histoire*, 32 (1954), pp. 1059-1074.

Hasluck, F. W., "Constantinata," in *Essays and Studies Presented to W. Ridgeway* (Cambridge, England, 1913), pp. 635-637.

Himly, F. J., "Y a-t-il emprise musulmane sur l'économie des états Européens du VIIIe au Xe siècle?" *Revue suisse d'histoire*, 5 (1955), pp. 31-81.

Ives, H. E., *The Venetian Gold Ducat and Its Imitations*, edited and annotated by Grierson, P. (New York, 1954).

Lopez, R. S., "The Dollar of the Middle Ages," *Journal of Economic History*, 11 (1951), pp. 209-234.

Miles, G. C., *The Coinage of the Umayyads of Spain* (New York, 1950).

Monneret de Villard, U., "La monetazione nell'Italia Barbarica," *Rivista Italiana di Numismatica*, ser. 2, 2 (1919), pp. 22-38, 73-112, 125-138.

Monroe, A. E., *Monetary Theory before Adam Smith* (Cambridge, Mass., 1923).

Montanari, G., *La zecca in consulta di stato*, in Graziani, A., *Economisti del Cinque e del Seicento* (Bari, 1913).

Nagl, A., "Die Goldwährung und die handelsmässige Geldrechnung im Mittelalter," *Numismatische Zeitschrift*, 26 (1895), pp. 41-258.

Naville, L., "Fragments de métrologie antique," *Revue suisse de numismatique*, 22 (1920), pp. 42-60.

Naville, L., "La livre romaine et le denier de la loi salique," *Revue suisse de numismatique*, 22 (1920), pp. 257-263.

Orsini, I., *Storia delle monete della Repubblica Fiorentina* (Florence, 1760).

Praj, G., "La moneta Piemontese ai tempi di Vittorio Amedeo I e Carlo Emanuele II," *Bollettino storico-bibliografico Subalpino*, 40 (1938), pp. 221-327.

Robertson, D. H., *Money* (Cambridge, England, 1948).

Rodolico, N., "Il sistema monetario e le classi sociali nel Medioevo," *Rivista Italiana di Sociologia*, 8 (1904), pp. 462-469.

Sánchez-Albornoz, C., "La primitiva organización monetaria de León y Castilla," *Anuario de historia del Derecho Español*, 5 (1928), pp. 301-345.

Sauvaire, M. H., "Matériaux pour servir à l'histoire de la numismatique et de la métrologie musulmanes," *Journal Asiatique*, ser. 7, 14 (1869), pp. 455-533; ser. 7, 15 (1880), pp. 228-277; ser. 7, 18 (1881), pp. 499-516; ser. 7, 19 (1882), pp. 23-163, 281-327.

Schrötter, F. von, *Wörterbuch der Münzkunde* (Leipzig and Berlin, 1930).

Serra, A., *Breve trattato delle cause che possono fare abbondare li regni di oro e di argento*, in Graziani, A., *Economisti del Cinque e del Seicento* (Bari, 1913).

Thesauro, G. A., *Tractatus novus de augmento ac variatione monetarum* (Turin, 1607).

Usher, A. P., *The Early History of Deposit Banking in Mediterranean Europe* (Cambridge, Mass., 1943).

Van Werveke, H., "Économie nature et économie argent," *Annales d'histoire économique et sociale*, 3 (1931), pp. 428-435.

Van Werveke, H., "Monnaie, lingots ou marchandises," *Annales d'histoire économique et sociale*, 4 (1932), pp. 452-468.

Whittlesey, A. E., *Principles and Practices of Money and Banking* (New York, 1948).

Wroth, W., *Catalogue of the Imperial Byzantine Coins in the British Museum* (London, 1908).

Zakythinos, D. A., *Crise monétaire et crise économique à Byzance du XIII au XV siècle* (Athens, 1948).

## STUDIES RELATING TO THE GENERAL SUBJECT

Aleati, G., "Biblioteche e prezzi di codici in Pavia nel tardo Medioevo," *Bollettino della Società Pavese di Storia Patria*, 49-50 (1951), pp. 99-107.

Bautier, R. H., "Les registres des foires de Champagne," *Bulletin philologique et historique* (1945), pp. 157-188.

Belgrano, L. T., "L'interesse del denaro e le cambiali appo i Genovesi dal sec. XII al XV," *Archivio storico Italiano*, ser. 3, 3, part I (1866), pp. 102-122.

Beveridge, W., *Prices and Wages in England from the Twelfth to the Nineteenth Century* (London, 1939).

Bloch, M., *La société féodale* (Paris, 1939).

Borlandi, F., "Biblioteche Pavesi del Quattrocento," *Bollettino della Società Pavese di Storia Patria*, 46 (1947), pp. 43-67.

Böuard, M. de, "Problèmes de subsistance dans un état médiéval: le marché et les prix des céréales au royaume angevin de Sicile, 1266-1282," *Annales d'histoire économique et sociale,* 10 (1938), pp. 483-501.

Bratianu, G. I., *Études byzantines d'histoire économique et sociale* (Paris, 1938).

Byrne, E. H., *Genoese Shipping in the Twelfth and Thirteenth Centuries* (Cambridge, Mass., 1930).

Caggese, R., *Roberto d'Angiò e i suoi tempi* (Florence, 1922-1930).

Catino, G. di, *Chronicon Farfense* in *Fonti per la storia d'Italia,* 33, 34 (1903).

Cibrario, L., *Della economia politica del Medioevo* (Turin, 1861).

Cipolla, C. M., "Il valore di alcune biblioteche nel Trecento," *Bollettino storico Pavese,* 7 (1944), pp. 5-20.

Cipolla, C. M., "In tema di trasporti medievali," *Bollettino storico Pavese,* 7 (1944), pp. 21-56.

Cipolla, C. M., "Finanze di borghi e castelli sotto il dominio Spagnuolo," *Bollettino storico Pavese,* 8 (1945), pp. 5-20.

*Codex Statutorum Magnifice Communitatis atque Diocesis Alexandrine* (Alessandria, 1547).

*Codice diplomatico della Università di Pavia* (Pavia, 1913-1915).

*Codice diplomatico Longobardo* in *Fonti per la storia d'Italia,* 62, 63 (1929, 1933).

Corti, G., editor, "Consigli sulla mercatura di un anonimo Trecentista," *Archivio storico Italiano,* 110 (1952), pp. 114-119.

De Capmany y de Montpalau, A., *Memorias historicas sobre la marina, comercio y artes de la antigua ciuidad de Barcelona* (Madrid, 1779).

Du Cange, C. D. F., *Glossarium mediae et infimae Latinitatis* (10 vols., Niort, 1883).

Hultsch, F. C., *Griechische und Römische Metrologie* (Berlin, 1882).

Karabacek, J. von, "Zur orientalischen Altertumskunde, II: die Arabischen Papyrusprotokolle," *Sitzungsberichte der philosophisch-historischen Classe der Kaiserlichen Akademie der Wissenschaften,* 161 (1909), pp. 1-103.

Lane, F. L., *Venetian Ships and Shipbuilders of the Renaissance* (Baltimore, 1934).

Lizier, A., *L'economia rurale dell'età prenormanna nell'Italia meridionale* (Palermo, 1907).

Ludwig, F., *Untersuchungen über die Reise-und Marschgeschwindigkeit im XII. und XIII. Jahrhundert* (Berlin, 1897).

Luzzatto, G. See Padovan, G.

Muratori, L. A., *Antiquitates Italicae Medii Aevii* (Milan, 1739).

Nesbitt, L. M., *Desert and Forest* (Bristol, 1955).

*Ordonnances des Roys de France de la troisième race*, edited by De Laurière, M., ɪ (Paris, 1723).

Padovan, G., "L'attività commerciale di un patrizio Veneziano del Quattrocento," *Rivista di storia economica*, 8 (1943), pp. 1-22.

Putnam, G. H., *Books and Their Makers during the Middle Ages* (London, 1896).

*Raccolta delle leggi della R. Casa di Savoia*, edited by Duboin, F. A. (Turin, 1851).

Renouard, Y., "La consommation des grands vins du Bourbonnais et de Bourgogne à la cour Pontificale d'Avignon," *Annales de Bourgogne*, 24 (1952), pp. 221-244.

Rodolico, N., *La democrazia fiorentina nel suo tramonto* (Bologna, 1905).

Sánchez-Albornoz, C., *Estampas de la vida en León durante el siglo X* (Madrid, 1926).

Sánchez-Albornoz, C., "El precio de la vida en el Reino Astur-Leonés hace mil años," *Logos: revista de la Facultad de filosofia y letras de la Universidad de Buenos Ayres*, 3 (1945), pp. 225-264.

Sapori, A., *Studi di storia economica medievale* (Florence, 1946).

Sieveking, H., "Studio sulle finanze genovesi nel Medioevo e in particolare nella Casa di San Giorgio," *Atti della Società Ligure di Storia Patria*, 35 (1905-1906).

*Statuta antiqua Abbatiae Corboliensis*, in Guerard, B. E., editor, *Le polyptyque de l'Abbé Irminon* (Paris, 1844).

*Statuto del Podestà*, edited by Caggese, R. (Florence, 1921).

Stein, E., "Untersuchungen zur spätbyzantinischen Verfassungs- und Wirtschaftsgeschichte," *Mitteilungen zur Osmanischen Geschichte*, 2 (1923-1925), pp. 1-62.

Ughelli, F., *Italia sacra* (Venice, 1720).

Vasco, G. B., *Osservazioni*, in Custodi, A., editor, *Scrittori Classici Italiani di Economia Politica*, 35 (Milan, 1804).

Verri, P., *Storia di Milano* (Milan, 1834).

Villani, G., *Istorie Fiorentine* (Milan, 1802-1803).

Winstedt, E. O., *The Christian Topography of Cosmas Indicopleustes* (Cambridge, England, 1909).

Wolff, P., *Commerce et marchands de Toulouse* (Paris, 1954).

INDEX

Abd el Aziz ibn Merwan, 17
Ab el Malek, 16ff.
account, denomination of, 50n.;
　money of, 39, 50n.; numerical
　unit of, 50n.; systems of, 50
accounting practices, 43
Alberti, B. degli, 36
Aleati, G., 59n., 63n.
Alessandria, 4
Allah, 17, 19
*altun*, 21n.
annuities, 64
Arabs, 16
"aristocratic money," 37
Armenia, 56
*ashrafti*, 21n.
*augustales*, 20

Balzani, U., 6n.
Barcelona, 31n., 48, 63
barter, 7, 11, 41
Bautier, R. H., 54n.
Bavaria, 11
Belgrano, L. T., 65n.
Bergman, E. von, 16n.
Beveridge, W., 52
*bezant*, 15n.
Bloch, M., 4n., 5n., 6n., 10n.
Bognetti, G. P., 6n.
Bohic, H., 62
books, price of, 57ff.
Borello, 60
Borlandi, F., 59n., 61n., 62n.
Bouard, 55n.
Bratianu, G. I., 13n.
Byrne, E. H., 55n.
Byzantine Empire, 16
Byzantines, 17, 18, 20

Caggese, R., 34n., 64n.
Calabria, Duke of, 64
Cannan, 26n.
Carli, G. R., 33n.
Carolingian Reform, 39
Carolingians, 11
Catino, G. di, 6n.
Charlemagne, 11
China, 57
Christians, 17, 21n.
Cibrario, L., 63n., 65n.
Cipolla, C. M., 8n., 14n., 15n.,
　32n., 46n., 54n., 57n., 60n.

*Codex Statutorum magnifice com-
　munitatis atque diocesis Alex-
　andriae*, 4n.
*Codice diplomatico longobardo*, 8n.
coinage, monopoly of, 31
coins, debasement of, 28, 32, 33ff.;
　demand for, 9, 10; shortage of,
　10; supply of, 8, 33; fractional,
　14
Conty, E. de, 62n.
convertibility, 31
Corbie, 53
*Corpus Juris*, 61
Corti, 65n.
Countess of Bloy, 61
creditors, 50
*cruzado*, 21n.
currency, international, 13, 14, 21;
　national, 14, 15

*dazii*, 54
debasement of coins, 28, 32, 33ff.
debtors, 50
De Buschis, P., 63
deflation, 35
De Capmany, A., 55n.
*Decretum Gratiani*, 61
De Laurière, M., 65n.
demand for coins, 9, 10, 11
*denarius*, 6, 38
denomination of account, 50n.
*dinar*, 16, 18ff., 20n., 21, 41
*dirham*, 16, 18, 19
distribution of income, 9
division of labor, 10, 42
dollar, 13
Dopsch, A., 4n., 8n., 11n.
Du Cange, C. D. F., 5n., 6n., 7,
　7n., 16n.
*ducato*, 21, 21n., 33, 37
*ducatone*, 37

economy, barter, 7; monetary, 7
Egypt, 17
El Kesay, 16
England, 26
entrepreneurs, 34f.
Evans, A., 50n.

Ferdinand (king), 64
Fiamberti, G. M., 59

73

## DATE DUE

| AP 12 8 | | | |
|---|---|---|---|
| 12/15/89 | | | |
| | | | |
| | | | |
| | | | |
| | | | |
| | | | |
| | | | |
| | | | |
| | | | |
| | | | |
| | | | |
| | | | |
| | | | |
| | | | |
| | | | |
| | | | |
| | | | |
| GAYLORD | | | PRINTED IN U.S.A. |